BLACK BEAUTIES

Published by The History Press
Charleston, SC
www.historypress.com

First published 2020

Manufactured in the United States

ISBN 9781467144827

Library of Congress Control Number: 2019952107

BLACK BEAUTIES

African American Pageant Queens
IN THE SEGREGATED SOUTH

KIMBERLY BROWN PELLUM, PhD

Foreword by Ericka Dunlap, Miss America 2004

THE
History
PRESS

1. Norvell Lee receiving award. 2. The King and his Court. 3. Homecoming Queen. 4. Joyce Burrows, Omega Queen. 5. Homecoming Parade, '52. 6. Christmas Sister Party. 7. Homecoming Dance, '52.

Toni Morrison is perched in a convertible (*bottom right*) in the 1953 homecoming parade and poses as part of the court at the official dance (*second from right*). *Moorland-Spingarn Research Center.*

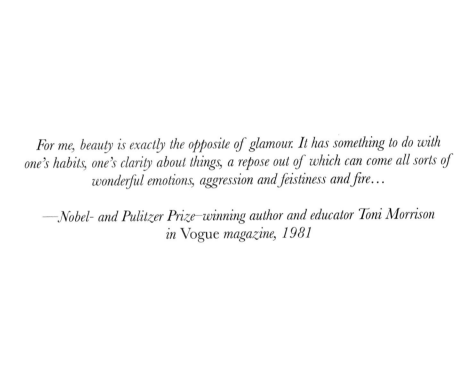

For me, beauty is exactly the opposite of glamour. It has something to do with one's habits, one's clarity about things, a repose out of which can come all sorts of wonderful emotions, aggression and feistiness and fire...

—Nobel- and Pulitzer Prize–winning author and educator Toni Morrison in Vogue *magazine, 1981*

CONTENTS

CONTENTS

FOREWORD

There she is, Miss America.
There she is, your ideal.
With so many beauties
She took the town by storm;
With her all American face and form.
And there she is!
Walking on air, she is;
Fairest of the fair,
She is, Miss America.

This final stanza of the renowned anthem "There She Is, Miss America," performed annually for over fifty years in front of a devout audience of several million onlookers and admirers in awe of the beautiful new Miss America, denotes a rather supremacist and abrupt dismissal of probability that, by chance, a Black woman could fit the bill as the ideal of American beauty. The refined, talented, well-spoken American beauty queen was instituted as a vital thread to the fabric of society in 1921 as a token of national pride, evoking unrelenting sentiment of honor similar to that of an Olympian, veteran or diplomat. As the song describes, this fair and noble beauty queen is a stunning, charming and endearing head-turner, but as history would have it, Black women were denied the opportunity to represent this ideal in the world's oldest beauty competition from 1921 to 1970.

Miss America 2004, Ericka Dunlap. *Courtesy Ericka Dunlap/ private collection.*

During that time, the Miss America pageant enforced "Rule 7," which was instituted during the 1930s, stating, "Contestants must be of good health and of the white race." This further inculcated the deliberate exclusion of Black contestants. It was unfathomable to the mediocre masterminds of pageantry, white males, that a Black woman could possibly inspire white women to be *more*. More beautiful, more talented, more intelligent, more appealing.

The significance of African American beauty queens during Jim Crow is a depiction of intrinsic symbolism and deep cultural pride that directly correlates with our instinctive, ancestral relationship to and admiration of authority as prominent African leaders: pharoahs, chiefs and queens. Even during periods when our civil liberties were being denied, the African American woman's innate comprehension of royal confidence, glamour and regalia continued to leave an indelible mark on American fashion, style and beauty that has irrefutably challenged the European standard.

For context's sake, the first African American contestant to appear on the coveted Miss America stage was Cheryl Hollingsworth, Miss Iowa 1970. Although she did not win, her presence and fortitude affixed a cornerstone of dignity and rightfulness in the due admission, promotion and coronation of Black contestants in Miss America and every other pageant to follow in its path. Her representation made a clear statement that Black women could compete and win at this game.

Whether a university queen, a scholarship program winner or any other varied permutation of pageantry, our Black beauty queens have served as a source of cultural pride that the entire African American community embraces, affirms and claims.

This body of work deeply resonates with me as the first and only African American woman to be crowned Miss Florida in the ninety-two-year history of the pageant and the seventh of nine African American Miss Americas to date. It is my sincere hope that Black women and girls for generations to come will celebrate themselves as fine examples of femininity, ladylike grace, elegance and eloquence in American society, with or without a crown. Because in truth, a beauty queen is a woman who rises to the occasion to utilize her influence in creating impact and legacy throughout her community. Any one of us can be a queen, if we simply decide to start where we are and allow the higher vibration of love and beauty to light the way.

—Ericka Dunlap, Miss America 2004

ACKNOWLEDGEMENTS

Many thanks to the team at The History Consultants LLC, especially Dr. Arlisha Norwood, whose professional insight is priceless. I appreciate the feedback provided by DeAnna Carpenter (dellesings. com), Dr. Ashley Preston (University of Florida) and Erin Washington (Spelman College). Special thanks to Sonja Woods, digitization specialist and archivist at Moorland Spingarn Research Center and research assistant Rhana Jones. My deepest gratitude is for my truest partner, Frederick James Pellum III. His encouragement is my survival and his description of me in the present is what I hope to become. If I had a thousand tongues, it wouldn't be enough to speak what enchantment and inspiration my baby girl brings to my life. I pray she feels my love eternally. The women interviewed for this project are the change agents of history. They redefine how and by whom history is told. I am honored they allowed me to narrate their experiences. Finally, this book is dedicated to Mary Faison, who personifies true beauty, in spirit and in deed. It would have been impossible to complete without her presence and support during such a life-changing time. To her, I am grateful always.

INTRODUCTION

American racism, both in practice and theory, has always linked human value to twisted notions of physical health and beauty. It has used white women as ornamental benchmarks to underscore the idea of superiority. Conversely, racism requires women of African descent to be marked by labels of promiscuity, ugliness and worthlessness. The history of mainstream American pageants, particularly Miss America and Miss USA, plainly reflects these imaginations with their limited presentations of fitness and loveliness.

Historically, pageants organized by African Americans, and heavily supported by the Black press, materialized remedies for American popular culture's persistent assault on African American women. Although actress Vanessa Williams's 1984 Miss America victory is an important moment by which African American participation in beauty contests is often framed, Black people in America have long lauded women of color within their own pageant productions. Similarly, Jackie Robinson's Major League career does not mark the beginning of Blacks in baseball. Suggesting otherwise is a Eurocentric and distorted view that disregards life and culture when not attached to white people. Black churches, colleges, social clubs, charitable groups, sororities and fraternal organizations have fashioned beauty competitions for more than a century. Moreover, African American women have formulated and continue to formulate their own treatise on beauty politics and public representation separate from the status quo.

Although these groups have established an extensive record of curating a profound Black beauty discourse, today U.S. media outlets still misrepresent Black beauty by omitting it, restraining it, caricaturizing it, exoticizing it, exceptionalizing it, appropriating it, commodifying it and regulating its form to skew toward Caucasian criteria. Magazines, books, blogs, television specials and movies continue to capitalize on Black women's complicated relationship to American beauty, often by relegating them to consumers in the beauty marketplace and listeners, rather than narrators, in serious beauty dialogue.

Furthermore, in the age of Michelle Obama, Oprah and Venus and Serena Williams, there remain debasing ideas about the possibilities of Black women, their images and, ultimately, their humanity. In 2016, Mayor Beverly Whaling of Clay, West Virginia, resigned after controversy arose concerning her commenting approvingly on a social media post that called then First Lady Obama "an ape in heels." The author of the post, Pamela Ramsey Taylor, director of the Clay County Development Corporation, a government-funded nonprofit, continued her celebratory response to Donald Trump's victory by stating, "It will be so refreshing to have a classy, beautiful, dignified First Lady back in the White House."[1] Should society have a response for such attitudes? It may be worthwhile to consider that convincing the world of a people's unattractiveness and attaching it to assumptions about morality congeals the recipe for justifying sweeping inequality as "deserving misfortune."

This book seeks to provide a retrospective for how Black society responded to beauty-centric racism during segregation. It amplifies the testimonies of African American beauty queens, pageant producers and curators of beauty culture. The oral interviews contained within reveal early examples of body positivity and the cultural and institutional factors that shaped African American contests. They also illuminate the nuances within their experiences in pageantry and everyday exchanges impacted by external and self-perceptions. The insider conversations on identity construction are certainly useful in today's era of social media, hypervisibility, personal branding and a surge in interest in the Black aesthetic.

Above all, this volume should serve as a record of existence of everyday African Americans who, regardless of racial climate, thought Black women were important enough to be crowned.

Chapter 1

"WE BRING YOU BEAUTY IN BRONZE"

*Early African American Pageant Tradition and the Revision
of a Limited Beauty Standard*

W hile slavery and the eras following presented awful traumas to
African American life, inequality failed to erase Black culture,
imagination and productivity. During bondage and after,
they created active and fascinating lives for themselves, despite their
circumstances. The same holds true for the age of Jim Crow, usually framed
by a one-hundred-year period after the Civil War up to 1968, when federal
legislation made discrimination and segregation illegal by way of the Civil
Rights Act, the Voting Rights Act and the Fair Housing Act. Even before
these major shifts in national history, however, Black life had persisted. In
fact, segregation helped sustain the continuity of an all-Black society, which
included worship centers, philosophical and artistic circles, educational
institutions, political groups and sports and leisure organizations. Galas,
balls and pageants, too, were common in certain Black social sets before
and after integration. Although public memory often associates African
Americans in pageants with actress Vanessa Williams's historic 1984 win
as Miss America, it is important to acknowledge the long history of events
produced *by* African Americans in honor of Black women. Black pageants,
having blended gender-based expectations with race work and glamour,
represent a dazzling chapter in pre-integration Black life.

Since the turn of the twentieth century, African American institutions and
organizations all over the United States have presented various contests and
pageants as a way to promote Black women as symbols of beauty and ideal
representations of the race. Historically, Black pageantry, heavily supported

The October 1948 cover of *Color* magazine featuring the queen of Florida A&M College and her court. *Dr. Emory Tolbert/Popular Black Media Collection.*

by the African American press, delivered remedies for American society's persistent assault on and erasure of African American women as worthy human beings. In 1914, the *Baltimore Afro-American Ledger* newspaper called its own Miss Hazel Macbeth "A Prize Beauty" in an esteemed recognition of her place as "one of the fifteen highest exponents of Negro Beauty."[2] The full report, about a large contest held in New York, showed how such competitions organized by African Americans worked to defend Black women from racist stereotypes, deepen the definition of beauty and advocate for a full measure of equality during Jim Crow.

AMERICA'S 100 MOST BEAUTIFUL NEGRO WOMEN

"The best part of beauty is that *which no picture can express."*—Bacon

Color Of Skin Not Important

AMONG the American Negroes are some of the most beautiful women in the world, and they have every possible complexion and facial contour that is conceivable among human beings. Colored women are truly "colored" women—their complexions range from the darkest brown to the most pronounced Caucasian, and their hair texture varies from the course and curly to the soft and silky types. A beautiful Negro woman may be of any color—dark-brown, light-brown, reddish-brown, red, or white, and the color of the skin is not as important as whether or not she has the charm, intellect, and kind of personality that augments her beauty. Admiration of beauty alone is not enough; for it is like admiring a house only because of its paint. Beauty has no one standard; for it thrives upon what the individual observer considers beautiful. What is beauty to one man may not be beauty to another. Tastes and reactions to beauty differ just as in the matter of deciding what color one's suit, dress, or the color of the automobile will be. This was markedly true among the judges who chose the 50 most beautiful Negro women.

Francis Quarles, the great English philosopher and author of the 16th century, clearly illustrated the variety of opinions on beauty when he said that "Socrates called beauty a short-lived tyranny; Plato, a privilege of nature; Theophrastus, a silent cheat; Theocritus, a delightful prejudice; Carneades, a solitary kingdom; Aristotle, that it was better than all the letters of recommendation in the world; Homer, that it was a glorious gift of nature, and Ovid, that it was a favor bestowed by the gods." These statements by a few of the greatest writers

that ever lived, show the many and different ways beauty appears to man. In short, there is no one standard for beauty, and no one group of judges can ever render a final decision as to which woman is the most beautiful. Whenever a beauty contest is held, and the final decisions are made by judges, their judgments represent what *they* believe to be the most beautiful—for there are always thousands of other women, equally as attractive, and equally as intelligent and personable, as those who are the final choices of the judges.

Beauty is not the exclusive property of the rich, nor is it the one virtue of the poor. It is indeed a free commodity that may be found in abundance among all occupational groups, whether sharecroppers, fruit-pickers, waitresses, saleswoman, office-girls, models or actresses. Wherever beauty is found in a woman, plus other desirable qualities, it is a thing of extreme advantage. Man's craving for a beautiful woman has had its impact in shaping the growth of civilization. For it has often been said that if Cleopatra's nose had been a half-inch shorter, the world we live in would be different today.

What Makes A Woman Beautiful?

There are certain attributes that most people regard as essentials for beauty. These attributes were discussed very appropriately by two of the judges participating in COLOR'S project, Artha Brown and Jon McCullough, co-owners of the Artha-Jon Studio in Cleveland, Ohio. These beauty experts said: "First there should be at least one outstanding feature that instantly attracts the eye. It may be the eyes, nose or mouth, the hair, the general facial contour, the legs, feet or hands, or the entire

From "America's 100 Most Beautiful Negro Women" editorial featured in *Color* magazine. *Dr. Emory Tolbert/Popular Black Media Collection.*

The contest was held at the Manhattan Casino as a feature event of the Autumn Exposition and Amusement Festival "given by colored New York."[3] The festival presented an array of "exhibits depicting the progress of the race along various lines since Emancipation" and opened on a Monday night with the reveal of the fifteen winners of the festival's beauty contest, which drew over two hundred submissions. Hazel Macbeth was one of the "Chosen Fifteen." Connecting pageantry to themes of humanity, the event featured booths that illustrated the achievements of people of color in the areas of dance, athletics and artistic composition. With a beauty contest as the opening ceremony, African American organizers demonstrated pageantry's value as a public engagement strategy, as well as Black people's resolve to include their physical attractiveness as an important factor in the larger definition of equality. The competition highlighted beauty as a possession of Black women. The winners were "those who are regarded as types of Negro belles, who would make any bronze-colored Adonis kneel and beseech their hand." The language suggests that not only were Black women deserving of marriage but also their loveliness created a yearning in men to extend a proposal.[4] The subtle statements overtly communicated the value of African American women as qualified wives rather than morally loose caricatures, as they had so often been treated during and after slavery.

Especially during Jim Crow, African American women did not appear in or receive positive coverage in mainstream national media, let alone get chosen as cover girls. Yet in 1923, the *Pittsburgh Courier* printed the pictures of a few of the "pretty and popular maids and matrons who entered the Beauty Contest to be held in connection with the American Legion picnic."[5] The cover of the *Negro American* magazine, in August 1927, showed a full-body print of Alice Stoglin as the winner of the San Antonio Bathing Revue.[6]

African American people continued to sustain and execute the agenda of affirming Black beauty, and Black media outlets remained committed to covering and sometimes sponsoring the tradition even during the 1930s, a period of severe economic decline across the nation. The Miss America pageant, established in 1921 as an Atlantic City promotional event designed to present the "Most Beautiful Bathing Girl in America," suspended its activities from 1928 until 1932 and again in 1934. Meanwhile, on July 30, 1931, the *Philadelphia Tribune*, an African American newspaper, publicized its collaboration with the Royal Theatre to stage a beauty pageant. The contest intended to locate the most beautiful colored girl in Philadelphia and promised a "grand reception" at the Strand Ballroom. Other prizes included a silver loving cup and an all-expenses-paid trip to New York City, where Miss

$5,000 including a free trip to Europe.

● For centuries women of color have made their mark on history. Beautiful Candace, Queen of Ethiopia; sensuous Cleopatra; Josephine, the creole belle who roped the man who conquered Europe—Napoleon. Negro women here have never received the recognition they deserve for their beauty. In old New Orleans, the quadroon ball on Orleans Street, used to be a kind of show-case for them. Back in the gay nineties, a St. Louis beauty, Melanie Macklin, won a nation-wide contest. And Gertrude Marshall, another St. Louisan, caused a tempest when a white newspaper found that the winner of its nation-wide beauty contest was Negro. Not long ago a Negro girl won the American Legion Beauty Contest in Philadelphia. But that's about all.

For our money, the beauty of Negro womanhood, with its varied skin-tones of copper, bronze, tan and olive, is matchless. OUR WORLD is convinced that now is the time to glorify the Negro woman and make her proud of her unusual beauty.

Lena Horne is a beautiful type and she has received her share of plaudits. But we feel that, in her way an unknown like 21-year-old Marine Ann Lamb (page 17) is no less beautiful. For Ann is that wonderful rarity—a dark woman with beautifully cut features. With it she has fine, even teeth, soft eyes, a radiant skin

and curly jet-black hair. All of this on a perfect frame.

Our World's Beauty Contest

For that matter we know that somewhere in these United States may exist Negro women many times more beautiful than Lena Horne. We want to find them. And you the public can help us. This issue officially starts the biggest talent hunt ever planned (we are proud to say) by any Negro publication — to find "the most beautiful Negro woman." *We want you to send in all the pictures of women you consider beautiful* — yourselves, your sisters, your friends. This contest is nation-wide. Every Negro woman is eligible. It will last until June 15, 1951 when, after a process of elimination, a panel of judges will choose *the most beautiful woman and a Court of Honor of nine runners-up.* For the lucky winner here are the fabulous prizes we offer:

★ A $1,000 wardrobe and a gown fashioned by one of Paris' greatest dress designers.

★ A trip to Paris, the Riviera, Rome and London, all expenses paid and with $500 pocket money for your shopping spree.

★ All prizes totaling at least $5,000.

The nine runners-up will get a free trip to New York where the winner will be officially announced at a gala party on Broadway's Astor Roof.

igne, 22-year old singer from Boston, Mass., is the "light-c" type. With soft dark-brown hair and clear complexion she's oking and obviously has pronounced Caucasian background.

Lena Horne is the "olive tan, sophisticated" type. Her beauty stems not only from her delicately modeled face and lovely dark hair but also from a cultured charm which men admire.

Mary Smith, New York model, is the "fair-to-white sexy" type. Stacked in the right places, Mary is the kind that attracts many wolf-calls. She's often mistaken for white, has no difficulty "passing."

An overview of contest details and prizes for the "Most Beautiful Woman in Our World" contest in 1950. *Dr. Emory Tolbert/Popular Black Media Collection.*

Grace Burroughs, Brooklyn, N.Y.; Dr. Mae McCarroll, New York and Mrs. Alfred Thomas, Detroit.

Also omitted were Ima Lou Pointer, Chicago, Janice Yates, Betti Mays, Marjul Cook, Sara Lou Harris, Sara E. Usher, Betty Jane Harmon, Charlotte Crump Poole, and Mrs. Marie Anderson (Sophie Tucker's maid).

More Beauties Next Month

Because of the overwhelming response received from our judges for this huge project, the editors of COLOR are forced to present a sequel to this compelling feature in our December issue. The latter issue of COLOR will contain the remaining fifty women who were not included this time due to the several reasons listed on Page 16. In addition, there will be many lovely ladies representing the southern and southwestern parts of the United States.

Thanks to the Judges

COLOR wishes to express sincere gratitude for the splendid cooperation shown by all of our judges (see Page 19 for pictures of judges), who sacrificed time from their daily work to assist in the monumental task of assembling "AMERICA'S 100 MOST BEAUTIFUL NEGRO WOMEN."

(Continued on next page)

MRS. ELEANOR DAILEY CYRUS, CHICAGO, ILLINOIS (above)—Mrs. Cyrus, the wife of Atty. Bindley C. Cyrus, a native of Bridgetown Barbados, B.W.I., is widely considered as the most beautiful Negro woman in the Chicago metropolitan area. She is the daughter of nationally prominent Dr. U. Grant Dailey.

LENA HORNE, LOS ANGELES, CALIFORNIA (below)—The most popular choice among the judges was Lena, one of the nation's favorites in radio, stage, screen and television.

PHILIPPA DUKE SCHUYLER, NEW YORK CITY—Philippa's intellectual achievements and musical genius, mark her as one of America's most gifted women. Today, at 17, she also takes her place among our most beautiful

While Lena Horne is ranked "Most Popular Among Judges" on *Color* magazine's beauty list, Philippa Schuyler is noted for her "intellectual achievements and musical genius." *Dr. Emory Tolbert/Popular Black Media Collection.*

Philadelphia would compete in the National Beauty Contest at the Savoy Ballroom and be presented to James J. Walker, mayor of New York City.[7] Baltimore's Black beauties, too, competed in a local contest in hopes of going to the same National Beauty Pageant at New York's famed Savoy, a Harlem Renaissance hot spot for African American socialites. Promoter Ike Dixon of Baltimore worked with organizer Lillian Reed to solicit participation from social clubs and lodges.[8] The *Afro American* even printed sizeable headshots of women representing "the two types of beauty which will vie for honors in the National Beauty Pageant" and asked subscribers, "Which style do you prefer?"[9] The public inquiry, again, evidenced pageantry as an outreach medium. Furthermore, readers were not only assured of the existence of Black beauty but its various incarnations as well.

Both the Philadelphia and the Baltimore competitions offered a $200 prize, which must have been enticing to anyone, especially Black girls, in the midst of the Great Depression. Financial incentives, a common feature of the contests, significantly influenced the participation of young African American women, many of whom contributed significantly to their families' livelihood or sought to acquire money for their own educational pursuits. "A beautiful contestant," seventeen-year-old Helen Lewis, landed the cover of Chicago's *Metropolitan Post* as it notified other potential contenders of the $100 award attached to the newspaper's own beauty pageant.[10] Additionally, many Black-sponsored contests openly embraced and celebrated Afrocentric features without apology, making the competitions even more attractive to women of color. A promotional advertisement for Chicago's Red Mill Beauties contest showed an array of twelve women, ranging in complexion, vying for the title of Miss Colored America.[11] In 1939, African American populations in Gary, Indiana, and East Chicago solicited nominations for "mayor" and "queen" of Bronzeville, a proud moniker for the towns' combined community of color. An advertisement specifically called for the "most beautiful and shapely girl."[12] "The contest manager and his bevy of assistants have scoured the entire city in search of alluring forms of every shape and type," the report read.[13] The grand prize was $100, and finalists were to wear summer formals on the night of the big affair. The paper assured entrants "at no time" would they be asked to "pose in bathing suits."[14] The guarantee underscored the extra precaution many African Americans took to secure the honor of their women, so often persecuted in the media and sexually assaulted in the reality of daily life as they rode on unsafe buses or worked as domestics in white homes during segregation.

African Americans also worked to demand the public integrity of Black women not only by applauding their appearance but also by placing special attentiveness on their intellectual prowess and cultural assets. Black periodical *Silhouette* chose Gladys Snyder as the "Glamour Girl of 1938" and professed talent, ambition and the brains to realize that ambition as prerequisites to earning such a title. It awarded her with a multipage spread in addition to an eight-by-eleven-inch portrait. The spread proudly announced Snyder as "a Los Angeles girl [who has] been training for the theatrical world since she was five years of age. Now at eighteen, she is a beautiful, modest young lady, who swings into a song or dance in a manner that captivates the hearts of an audience."[15] It predicted, "She will be hailed as a new star among the stars," while *Time* magazine, a white-run publication, had called Black starlet Josephine Baker a buck-toothed Negro wench just three years earlier. Such degrading remarks in reference to Black women were normal, making narratives like those featured in *Silhouette* all the more unique and necessary.

Silhouette touted itself in bold letters as "Glorifying Bronze Beauty" and being the only pictorial publication "dedicated to the glorification of the world's loveliest women." Editors asserted, "In *Silhouette*, The Charm and The Beauty of the Race is Displayed for Your Appreciation. From Every Part of Our Nation We Bring You Beauty in Bronze!" It met its promise and positively showcased women of color, ranging in age, throughout its pages. One issue featured a sizeable portrait with the caption "Gaudet Girl Reserves Court of the Gaudet Normal and Industrial School of New Orleans." The group of nineteen African American youths posed regally as they sat on thrones, wore crowns and held scepters—the boys in bow ties and the girls in floor-length dresses.[16] The same issue included images from the Los Angeles Annual Beauty Show, held at the main auditorium of the commodious Elks building in the heart of the Negro business district. African American teenage girls smiled as they modeled ornate dresses and various coiffeurs. Several "charm girls" from Texas also made the publication and received headshots and printed recognition of their academic achievements, sorority affiliations and service to families and communities. The magazine stated, "Miss Heddie Edith Branch, of Port Arthur, Texas, will be a senior at Prairie View College this fall, where she will continue her studies in music and home economics. She assists her father in his drug store in her spare time."

As a widely practiced community custom, Black pageants disputed the Jim Crow and eugenics ideologies of World War II, which deemed people of color as deficient. Miss America's history of itself contends, "In those

This Miss Bishop State article appeared next to superstar Dorothy Dandridge in 1954.
Chronicling America/Library of Congress.

Miss Dillard's photo tops the pages in 1940. *Chronicling America/Library of Congress.*

The *Detroit Tribune* featured Miss Southern University on December 7, 1946. *Chronicling America/Library of Congress.*

Left: Miss Tuskegee Institute Hattie Grimmett, 1940–41. *Archives at Tuskegee University.*

Right: Miss Tuskegee Institute Bobbie Goodson, 1947–48. *Archives at Tuskegee University.*

years, the image of Miss America, with her small-town persona, youth and energy, was becoming enshrined in the nation's imagination as America's ideal woman."[17] All of the organization's winners since its inception in 1921 were white. If that contest was the barometer, African American women were not worthy of consideration concerning American beauty. In fact, since the 1930s, Miss America had institutionalized its infamous Rule 7, which contractually obligated local state sponsors to ensure its decree that every "contestant must be in good health and of the white race."[18] Furthermore, even earlier in its history, Miss America welcomed its first Black participants: men and women depicted as slaves who performed a musical selection.[19] It was obvious that without an alternative, white beauty would continue to operate as the social norm and the only beauty that mattered.

Black people decided to enshrine their own women as ideal. By the time Miss America formalized Rule 7, Howard University, a Black college located in Washington, D.C., and founded in 1867, had been formally celebrating African American women via its May Festival pageant and other titles for many years. The May Festival underscored noble virtues of Black women, which was a departure from the apartheid customs practiced in the nation's capital. The majority of the city's public facilities, schools and housing were segregated, and internationally known opera singer Marian Anderson was infamously denied the stage at Constitution Hall by the Daughters of the American Revolution. Meanwhile, in the Black section of the same city, Howard presented its fifteenth annual May Festival on Friday, May 31, 1941.

A portion of a report on the event read, "The [May] Queen, a member of the senior class, was selected by the entire student body on the basis of the following criteria: Honorable character, scholarship, leadership and service."[20] Not only were less superficial qualities brought into focus, but both young college women and seasoned community women were honored, which, again, expanded the idea of beauty beyond age and appearance. Additionally, beauty was linked to academic achievement and meaningful civic involvement, which in many ways separated black pageants and contests from its white mainstream counterparts. The University May Queen report outlined how the festival showcased successful students at Howard across the disciplines.

The students representing the various schools and colleges of the university were chosen from a group of ranking students in each of the following schools and colleges: the Graduate School, the College of Liberal Arts, the School of Music, the School of Engineering and Architecture, the School of Religion, the School of Law, the College of Medicine, the College of Dentistry and the College of Pharmacy.[21]

Most Black colleges, usually located in the Deep South, had queens by the time they had athletic programs, as early as 1900. As a result, good academics and the expectation that these queens maintained good standing were built into these titles and positions. On the other hand, Miss America did not integrate its first scholarship into its

TWO PRETTY BROWN-SKIN CO-EDS—Betty Morgan (top photo) wears the crown of "Miss Wilberforce State College," and Rose Marie Tayen, dark skinned west coast beauty, is one of the most popular and attractive at Wilberforce University

Brown-skinned college queens get national publicity in 1950. *Dr. Emory Tolbert/Popular Black Media Collection.*

29

program until 1945, which only then began to spark the interest of more women concerned with college. Beyond showcasing African American women's academic achievements, Black pageants also ushered them into some of society's more influential circles. Through a multitude of disenfranchisement tactics exercised by white supremacists and legalized by the inaction of federal government, Jim Crow society demanded African Americans be essentially shut out of American politics and advantageous social cache. Therefore, these community-organized contests and elections functioned as conduits to some level of acquaintance to and acceptance within the larger society. For instance, when the Black community of Gary, Indiana, elected its first "Mayor of Bronzeville" and "Miss Bronzeville" beauty queen, the two were "dined and banqueted by governors, city mayors, and members of the chamber of commerce."[22] While they may not have wielded any concrete political power, the positions solidified them as diplomats representing the African American community. Dubbed the "first Negro beauty queen to see Paris," nineteen-year-old Iris Smith, Miss Harlem, won a fabulous seven-day Paris vacation, which included visitations to Jaques Fath and Christian Dior fashion salons. "She saw all the city's famed landmarks, was photographed for the newspapers, magazines, newsreels, and television. At the City Hall, she received the French Medal of Honor from Mayor Bernard Lafay, and U.S. ambassador C. Douglas Dillon gave her the keys to the U.S. Embassy." At the famed Moulin Rouge Café, she enjoyed a performance by Hazel Scott and greeted the starlet musician and her husband, Adam Clayton Powell.[23]

At Howard, student leaders like the May Queen found opportunities to interact with Black dignitaries. The 1940 festival program listed as a faculty representative Dr. Ralph Bunche, the first Black man to earn a PhD in political science from American University and a member of President Franklin Roosevelt's "Black Cabinet" advisory board. It also cited Mrs. Mordecai Johnson, first lady of the university, as ceremonial hostess and Lois Mailou Jones as designer of the official crown and consultant to the event.[24] Certainly, students' interactions with such highly distinguished persons broadened their perspectives and future possibilities.

Jones, an internationally acclaimed Harlem Renaissance artist whose work was featured at the Smithsonian Art Museum, sketched the crown's design in an elaborate arrangement of sapphires and rhinestones to reflect the school colors, blue and white. Her ornate illustration included an "HU" monogramed medallion resting in the center of the headpiece just before it ascended to its highest point, about four inches from the forehead. Most

The first-ever Miss Wilberforce made headline news on November 2, 1940. *Chronicling America/Library of Congress.*

10 MOST BEAUTIFUL NEGRO WOMEN—Continued

The "most beautiful Negro woman" may be you. There are no limits and everybody is eligible.

Jane White, daughter of NAACP sec'y Walter White, is the "light, entertaining" type. An actress in her own right, she enhances personality with stylish clothes.

Valencia Butler of Cleveland, O., is the "light, frag-

Edith Chandler of Miami, Fla., is the "sweet, nut-brown" type. College-trained Red Cross worker, she has soft, appealing face and warm, sun-tanned skin.

Carmen de Lavallade is the "graceful, creole" type. She's a 17-year-old product of Los Angeles and a talented dancer. The exotic, Latin-quality in her face comes naturally. Her parents are from New Orleans and she loves French.

Above: The November 1950 issue of *Our World* declared, "The most beautiful Negro woman may be you. There are no limits and everyone is eligible." *Dr. Emory Tolbert/Popular Black Media Collection.*

Right: Miss Tuskegee Institute Thelma Neal, 1954–55. *Archives at Tuskegee University.*

likely a very expensive piece, the crown was paid for by several women's organizations each year. In 1947, Alpha Kappa Alpha sorority, Delta Sigma Theta sorority, Sigma Gamma Rho sorority, Zeta Phi Beta sorority, the Women's League, Howard Women's Alumni Club and Howard Women's Faculty Club were each listed as sponsors. The Men's Dormitory Council subsidized the queen's bouquet.

That same year, the ceremony's theme rested on the preamble of the United Nations. The British Embassy, the Chinese Embassy, the French Embassy, the South African Embassy, the Spanish Embassy, the Swedish Embassy and the Pan American Union each donated their respective banners for the formal presentation of flags. Attendees included Howard notables such as President Mordecai Johnson and Dorothy Porter, the widely respected university archivist and bibliographer who represented the Faculty Wives Club. The special stage construction commissioned by the event's organizers and professional makeup artists recruited for the honorees reiterated how seriously, and to what lengths, African American institutions labored to celebrate African American women, even during times of economic challenge.

Underscoring the relationship between beauty and equality, prominent race leaders attached their names to pageantry. In 1945, congressman Reverend Adam Clayton Powell's face appeared on the flier advertising the International Sepia Beauty Contest held in Windsor, Canada.[25] Like the New York Autumn Festival held at the beginning of the century, it was one highlight in a string of events celebrating Emancipation. Powell was invited as a special guest, possibly a speaker, the day before the beauty and talent competition, which was introduced in 1931 and continued to thrive throughout the 1960s as a cherished tradition for African Canadians. In 1941, the group recognized its 108th Emancipation celebration and offered Miss Sepia International $500. The title, and acceptance of Black American contestants, is evidence of the community's recognition of the African Diaspora and their part in it. It hinted at the variety in Black beauty.

Clubs, civic groups and organizations across the United States hosted pageants throughout the 1950s. Many were linked to social welfare initiatives. One of the largest and most illustrious was given by the Shriners, an African American Masonic fraternity. The Ancient Egyptian Arabic Order Nobles of the Mystic Shrine expected more than eight thousand delegates and visitors from 142 temples in as many cities for its 1951 annual convention.[26] Principal business included discussions on the progress of the Shriners' Tuberculosis and Cancer Research Foundation Inc., which had

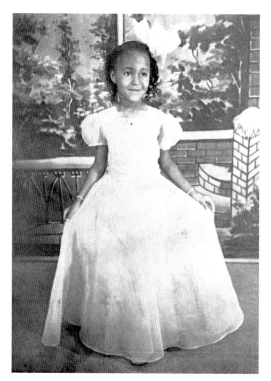

Nine-year-old May Day queen
Johnella Reid Bell in Tallahassee,
Florida. *Florida Memory/State Library
and Archives of Florida.*

raised $35,000 the previous year for medical research. The fifth annual talent and beauty pageant featuring twenty young ladies from various sections of the country also made the agenda. The organization financially awarded all the participants and extended to the first-place winner a scholarship in the amount of $1,500. The following year, the Shriners offered the sizeable scholarship again and an expense-free trip to the national finals in Indianapolis. An organization of men, they conveyed traditional American notions of womanhood and beauty in their proclamation of rules that stated, "Generally, the participants must be single and never have been married; must not be less than 17 years nor more than 25 years of age."[27] Conceivably, the age restriction might have denoted the group's charitable intentions to provide financial aid for college-bound young people. Nonetheless, the clear guidelines emphasized the insufficiency of a pretty face alone. They read, "Contestants must have talent, such as singing, dancing, dramatic reading, modeling, drawing, designing, etc."[28] Service connected to tuberculosis research remained chief in purpose for the pageant in 1953. The Prince Hall affiliation of the Shriners luminously publicized the now annual affair. Part of a lengthy newspaper announcement vowed to ticket buyers:

The 1956 Miss **Marracci** announcement in the *Detroit Tribune. Chronicling America/Library of Congress.*

Some of the finest talent in the Midwest, and under the best instructors
of this area, they will be presented between the participating contestants,
who will display the latest creations in afternoon wear, evening wear, and
bathing attire, no effort has been spared in preparing this program, and it
promises to be one of the most gala affairs of the Spring Season.[29]

The appeal concluded by reminding readers of the fraternity's community work. It sought to continue the implementation of its nationwide physical examination initiative, including provisions for lung cancer X-rays and pap smear testing. The group resolved that the fight against cancer "is ours and we have accepted the challenge to do all in our power with the help of Almighty God and the help of our fellowman, and our fellowman can help by supporting the Shrine Talent and Beauty Pageant."[30]

In 1954, Diahann Johnson placed second in the national contest. Johnson later eclipsed the winner, Alma Elaine Sisco, in fame as she ultimately became known as Diahann Carroll, a Broadway sensation who also starred in the African American breakthrough film *Carmen Jones* that same year. *Jet* magazine reported that she "typifies the talent-laden beauties who come from key cities around the nation to vie for the coveted title of 'Queen' of the Ancient Egyptian Arabic Order of Nobles of the Mystic Shrine, in a contest which boasts the richest rewards and most elaborate promotion of any Negro beauty contest in the U.S."[31] Now "a resplendent affair" receiving national headlines, with scholarships going to the top five contestants totaling $4,000 and a promotion and production cost of $7,000, the Shriners pageant continued the Black tradition of pampering and protecting its women. "From Los Angeles to Boston, some 20–25 girls are brought yearly to the convention site (their transportation and that of a chaperone paid for by the body) to be wined and dined for the weeklong convention at the expense of (and in the true style) the fun-loving Shriners."[32]

Other associations and institutions, particularly African American fraternities, schools and civil rights groups, continued to shape 1950s Black middle-class social engagement through their implementations of pageantry. The Spirit of Cotton Makers' Jubilee contest, for instance, continued in the theme of promoting the multifaceted quality of young African American women and introducing them as ambassadors to worthy causes. The Memphis Cotton Makers' Jubilee was an annual weeklong celebration, of which Father of the Blues W.C. Handy was the national honorary president, designed to take a "positive approach toward informing America of the Negro's active participation in the production, cultivation,

Left: Miss Marracci announced in the *Detroit Tribune*, July 11, 1959. *Chronicling America/Library of Congress.*

Right: The *Detroit Tribune* covered the Shriners Pageant in May 1955. *Chronicling America/ Library of Congress.*

and development of cotton, its usages, and the innumerable products and by-products of cotton."[33] The wearer of the title "Spirit of Cotton Makers' Jubilee" promoted cotton fashions and the general industry. "These fabulous fabrics are all furnished by the National Cotton Council of America."[34] The contest incorporated an educational element within its "Charm Clinic." It was built in as "the mechanism for giving to the candidate that feeling of security for better living.…Charm and Beauty are emphasized as a matter of inner spiritual radiance as it is of outward perfection. One's mental thinking affects one's looks.…The spirit feeds the soul, the emotional and mental backgrounds reflect in the face."[35]

The Cotton Makers' Jubilee itself was a response to Jim Crow. It was established in 1935 as the Black answer to the Memphis Cotton Carnival, which had denied participation to African American Memphians. Dr. Ransom Q. Venson, an African American dentist from Rapides Parish, Louisiana, who trained at Meharry Medical College in Nashville, founded the jubilee. Deeply familiar with the practices of southern Jim Crow, Venson set up his

bouy either in form or grace or movement. But if a woman is the possessor
of all these attributes and is devoid of
personality, charm and intellect, then
nature has wasted her gifts." The latter is also what John Robert Powers,
internationally known beauty expert
had in mind when he said his selec-
tions of the "most beautiful Negro
women in America" were made "keep-
ing in mind our idea of beauty . . .
the natural girl or woman . . . posses-
ing an inner glow as well as outer
glow—which is from within."

On these pages are photographs of
twenty-seven women from many parts
of the United States. They represent
what COLOR's judges regarded as the
most beautiful Negro women. But
many of the women nominated are
not shown because of three reasons:

Some pictures came in too late to
be included; a few women were
pleased to be nominated, but did not
care for the publicity; and others
were omitted because of the space
limitations of this feature.

These are the remaining twenty-
three beautiful women who were
named by the judges and whose pic-
tures are not shown: Joyce Thomp-
son, St. Louis; Florida Whiteside,
New York; Mrs. Marva Louis, Chi-
cago; Helen Ritchie, New York; Mrs.
Dorothy Leedie, Bronx, N.Y.; Atty.
Elsie Austin, formerly of Cincinnati,
O., but now of Washington, D.C.
Others include Judge Jane Bolin, New
York; Betty Dorsey, formerly of
Pittsburgh, now of New York; Mrs.
Douglass Henry, Kasota Pl., Cincin-
nati; Marian Bruce, New York; John-
nie Lee Batt Yancy, Atlanta, Ga.;

MRS. LOUISE FOSTER MOSELEY, NEW YORK CITY (above)—Mrs. Moseley is not only one of New York's most beautiful women, but she is also very active with the Harlem Council Committee and serves as chairman of its special events committee, and is head of its group of volunteer workers. Mrs. Moseley was born in Washington, D.C., and attended Northwestern University.

MRS. ETHEL RAMOS HARRIS, NEW KENSINGTON, PENNA. (below)—Mrs. Harris, a pianist-vocalist, is a popular star of radio, stage and television. She was born in Brazil, S.A., and is now a citizen of the U.S.A. She is considered by many as one of the most beautiful and best dressed women in Pittsburgh (New Kensington is a suburb of Pittsburgh).

JOHNNIE MAE BOMAR, AKRON, OHIO—Miss Bomar achieved national prominence when she won the Ohio Shriners beauty contest at Cleveland in 1948 and went on to represent Ohio in the finals. She has been a profes-sional photographer for almost three years.

Johnnie Mae Bomar, from Akron, won the Shriners Beauty Contest in Cleveland, Ohio, in 1948. *Chronicling America/Library of Congress.*

own event and served as director of the jubilee until his death in 1970. His wife, Ethyl, served as the first queen in 1935 and as director from 1970 to 1985. "The many activities of the Cotton Makers' Jubilee, particularly the selection of a King and Queen and a Royal Court, the organization provided an opportunity for African Americans in Memphis to enjoy their own parties, parades and celebrations."[36]

Organizers believed in a deeper meaning of beauty concept and not only sought such qualities in their participants but also endeavored to help develop them. Detailed pageant literature read, "To be truly beautiful, the candidate learns that one must think right, live right and be right inside one's own mind and soul."[37] The regulations emphasized service to the jubilee, the participant's college and the nation in an admirable manner. "It is not enough that she possess a pleasing or dynamic personality, but it must be penetrating and lasting as to pave the way for future representatives."[38] The guidelines for contestants addressed both physical expectations as well as those concerning conduct and presentation. An intense and detailed list of requirements read:

1. She must be photogenic. Some pretty girls look sad when a camera gets through with them, and such are not "Spirit" material.
2. She must have a good figure since she will be photographed in playsuits.
3. And she must be a good model. We cannot have a girl so short or so heavy or with such neck and shoulders that she'll set back the play clothes.
4. The "Spirit" must be physically strong—not that she will be required to do anything strenuous—but simply that six weeks of fast, tight schedules and the strain of meeting thousands of people agreeably call for good health.
5. Since her appearances will be necessarily brief, she's got to have a personality people like right away, rather than the sort that appeals to you after you've known her for a longer period of time.
6. She must not be moody or overly sensitive. She must work with civic committees, news personalities, fashion coordinators, etc. and that requires a certain toughness.
7. She must have culture and refinement. She should come from a home that other members of her family who join her on any

occasion will be a welcome asset. Surely, the Board of Judge wishes this to be treated with delicacy.

8. She should also have special talents, since these are frequently referred to, and in the past have consisted of charming voices, ability with musical instruments, and the like. She has other barriers to hurdle but this gives you an idea of the requirements.[39]

In 1955, the Spirit of Cotton Makers' Jubilee chose the personification of these qualities in "vivacious Joyce Alvia McClinton, a 17-year-old freshman at Arkansas A&M College," as the traveling emissary of charm, cotton fashions and goodwill. Playing the marimba, she beat out other young ladies from Bethune-Cookman College of Daytona Beach, Florida; Tennessee A&I University of Nashville; Lane College of Jackson, Tennessee; Grambling College of Grambling, Louisiana; Mississippi Vocational College of Ita Bena; and Texas Southern of Houston, all historically Black institutions. The daughter of Little Rock's Arkansas Democratic Voter's Club president, McClinton visited several major U.S. cities such as New York and Washington, D.C., in addition to Havana, Cuba, and Port-au-Prince, Haiti, as "ambassador of goodwill to the Jubilee, Memphis, the Negroes of the Mid South, and the cotton industry."[40]

Not only did African American colleges have queens, but the campus organizations within the universities often selected their own "Miss" honorees too. There are nine historically Black Greek-lettered organizations (BGLOs) that make up the National Pan-Hellenic Council. Collectively, they are known as the "Divine Nine." Of the nine, six were founded at Howard University and eight were established between 1906 and 1922.

In 1952, the Omega Psi Phi fraternity at Howard hosted a colorful costume ball, described by *Jet* magazine as "one of the top social events of the year" on campus. Patricia Adams was crowned queen, and the festive costumes included a ruffle-bedecked southern belle, a goateed Kentucky colonel, a Mandarin princess and a Bengal lancer.[41] The basileus of the Omegas of Pittsburgh presented Carnegie Tech coed Jeri Jackson with a glitzy crown and red roses at their Mardi Gras soiree.[42] The Elks, the historical lodge, also incorporated pageants into their most prominent activities. They held a beauty contest in conjunction with their national convention in Chicago, at which they chose pretty manicurist Gertrude Straughter over eleven other contestants in 1954. In New York, "Glamorous Nancy Gladstone was crowned Queen of Clubs at the fourth annual Queen of Clubs Ball sponsored by the Friends of the Northside Community Center in the Savoy

Color magazine's "America's Most Attractive College Queens," all from historically Black colleges and universities, in 1950. *Dr. Emory Tolbert/ Popular Black Media Collection.*

Left: Miss Bethune Cookman College on the front page of the *Detroit Tribune*, December 15, 1951. *Chronicling America/Library of Congress.*

Right: College queens were regular society features in Black newspapers and magazines. Here, Miss Bethune Cookman and court in 1951. *Chronicling America/Library of Congress.*

Ballroom."[43] Gladstone reaped the usual benefits of these social titles on her trip to Los Angeles.

The popularity of beauty programs among African Americans reinscribed respectability, poise and high style as standards held dearly by the community. The activities surrounding the pageants offer insight into these cultural mores. For example, Vernealure Patterson won an abundant bouquet of roses and a crown as Miss Charm at the culmination of Lemoyne College's annual charm clinic.[44] The Rue-Jac School of Modeling graduated twenty-five young students in its fourth annual commencement/ fashion show held at the Parkway Ballroom, where Mary Broomfield was crowned queen of the school for 1952.[45] In New Orleans, "in a panorama of pageantry of color, 26 graciously poised crescent City debutantes made their bow to society at the 56th Annual Original Illinois Debutante Ball."[46] It, too, met the prerequisites of pomp for which fine Black soirees and presentations of beauty had become known. "The theme of the carnival spirited affair, staged at the Rosenwald Memorial Center was the 'Doges of Venice' with Dr. A.C. Terrance of Opelousas, Louisiana, acting as Doge. Champagne bubbled freely and private parties in separate rooms of the center kept pace with the main ballroom activity." Two "maids of honor" attended to the queen of the ball, who was "gowned in yards of foamy white tulle."[47] African Americans curated these splendid affairs year after year, establishing their own traditions and communicating their own ideas about Black women.

Chapter 2

"THEY DIDN'T HAVE MANY QUEENS MY COLOR"

Colorism, Community and Growing Up during Jim Crow

Although Black-sponsored pageants had healthy intentions to encourage African American women and promote beauty as part of the larger racial uplift agenda, colorism substantially affected African American beauty culture and its outgrowth of events and programs. The preoccupation with shade that penetrated some aspects of African American culture did not begin or end with pageantry. The intersectionality of class, complexion and community had been observable in the everyday lives of African Americans since slavery. White supremacy influenced how African Americans attempted to survive and succeed in the United States, sometimes resulting in the formation of lines of demarcation among themselves. Even after slavery, state-sanctioned racism produced housing and job discrimination, in addition to constant threats to personal safety. This was enough reason for some Blacks to seek exemption from such treatment by separating themselves by color. Some who had light enough complexions chose to "pass" by living as white persons, essentially opting out of trauma caused by bigotry. Most African Americans, however, were unable to mask their skin color, regardless of gradation. Most, from honey yellow to the deepest brown, found themselves existing in the realities of Jim Crow.

In fact, Jim Crow's significance as the official legal code of the United States is tied to the case of a very light-skinned man of mixed descent who challenged the public transportation policies of the Deep South. The Comité des Citoyens, a civil rights group formed by African Americans in New Orleans, assigned Homer Plessy, an "octoroon," the task of contesting

No Color Bias in Attractive Co-ed Selections

IN response to COLOR'S request that photos be sent of their most attractive co-eds, we found that America's Negro colleges demonstrated no preference for lighter women. None of the colleges contacted was aware of what disposition would be made of the lovely ladies. On these two pages are seven attractive co-eds ranging in color from a dark brown to a very light complexion. Violette Collins, (left photo, above) freshman at Fisk University, Nashville, Tenn., is a lovely dark-brown miss. Vivian Chappelle, (right photo above) is a light-skinned co-ed from S. C. State A & M college, Orangeburg, S.C. Fannie Mae Wilson (bottom photo on left) a pretty dark-brown freshman, was voted "The Most Beautiful Co-ed" on Alabama A & M College campus in Normal, Ala. Lovely Mayme R. Brooks (below photo on right) an attractive brown-skinned queen, was chosen "Miss Municipal College" at Louisville Municipal College in Louisville, Ky.

Above: This 1950 article discusses beauty inclusivity at Black colleges. *Dr. Emory Tolbert/ Popular Black Media Collection.*

Right: *Our World* described Mildred Smith as "light brown, sparkling" in 1950. *Dr. Emory Tolbert/ Popular Black Media Collection.*

Mildred Joann Smith, who's a product of Cleveland, O., is the "light brown, sparkling"

Louisiana's separate-car law, which forbade Blacks from sitting among Anglo persons aboard trains. On June 7, 1892, Plessy purchased a first-class ticket and sat in the white section. Although he looked European, he was arrested, and the case made its way to the Supreme Court. In 1896, the Supreme Court ruled in *Plessy v. Ferguson* that racial segregation was constitutional. The ruling validated and federalized state laws that sought to reinstitute racial order in the South.

As evidenced by the *Plessy* case, color lines bore considerable weight, not in just trivial realms such as definitions of attractiveness, but also in more palpable considerations that affected people's livelihoods. For instance, "the earliest Black clerks of the Freedmen's Savings and Trust Company established a closed-membership bank ring, which evolved into the Lotus

Club, a members-only organization limited to fair skinned men." The network circulated industry job opportunities and accompanying money among its members, extending no welcome to darker people. Wealthy banker W.E. Matthews served as the group's "captain general" and promoted the right of mulattoes to be recognized as a distinct race and higher caste.[48]

Color-consciousness infected education, too. In Washington, D.C., although not officially sanctioned to do so, Dunbar High School catered to pale African Americans and provided high-quality learning by way of its faculty, several of whom had PhDs from Ivy League universities. Many darker African Americans attended Armstrong High School, which focused on trade skills. Meanwhile, it was not uncommon for Dunbar students to pass and enjoy theaters and restaurants frequented by whites. Dunbar was known for placing its graduates into prestigious universities, including Howard, Harvard and Yale. The few dark students who attended had to be exceptional. A 1948 alumna remembered, "You'd see a dark Black going to Dunbar and you'd say, 'Gee, you must be smart if you go here.'"[49]

Still, mixed-race heritage wasn't enough to secure a first-rate education in most other parts of the segregated South. In 1953, the Alabama Supreme

Linda Grace Brown as Miss Union High School in 1964. *Brown family collection.*

Court upheld a ruling that prevented a seven-year-old "Creole" boy from attending a white school. State authorities determined "Creole" to mean "part Negro," and thus, protests from white parents led to the boy's dismissal, although his father formally testified that he had attended white churches and had "associated intimately" with white persons all of his life.[50]

The weight and complexity of color in some Black communities was heavy and burdensome. How people conceptualized beauty at even the most basic levels reflected these complications. Linda Grace Brown, who became a high school beauty queen in her teens, faced the strange effects of colorism very early. Born in 1946, she remembered getting a black doll at a time when they were unusual:

> *One year, Mama, or Santa Clause, bought me for Christmas a dark-skinned doll that had on a little white suit and he had red lips and he was crying. I fell in love with that doll immediately. He was just my doll. For Christmas she dressed me up and she took me to visit a* [African American] *lady who had just had a baby. She looked at my doll and just fell out laughing. She said, "That's the ugliest doll I've ever seen in my life!" And she said it again! It hurt my feelings. I said, "Well, my baby is no uglier than yours!" And I can remember until this day my mother did not know what to do. She said, "I think it's time for us to go," and she put on her coat, and we left.*[51]

The ways in which some African Americans, including the adult lady mocking the child's doll, had internalized the notion of color-based appeal often showed up publicly. There were many examples of openly and unapologetically endorsed trends of complexion-based discrimination. Black pageants sometimes put these preferences on full display. *Jet* magazine commented on the topic in a 1953 editorial titled "The Truth About Beauty Contests" that plainly quipped:

> *Most Negro beauty contest winners usually turn out to be fair-skinned girls. Promoters explaining that they are striving for "what the public wants most," get rid of the contestants with dark skins early in the competition. As a result, when the final selections are made, the girls still in the running range from a light brown to near white. This fact has been the cause of considerable bitterness among dark girls seeking beauty queen honors. Their supporters and friends frequently charge that the contests are "fixed" or "rigged" so that the eventual winner will be a girl with a light complexion and "good hair."*[52]

A THING OF BEAUTY IS A

CHARLOTTE WESLEY
"Miss Collegiate America"

BEAUTY SECTION

Miss Charlotte Wesley was selected in 1941 as "Miss Collegiate America" in the Delta Phi Delta National Beauty Contest. The runner-up was also a Howardite, Doris Brown, on the far right. Typical of "The Capstone's" beauteous co-eds, are these charming young ladies that follow, some elected queens and all of them popular selectee queens, flowers of studious attraction that adorn the branches and thorns that make college life.

SELENA EDWARDS   HARRIET PEARSON   ELOISE DOWNING
"Miss Hilltop Homecoming"

Beauties at Howard University in 1941. *Moorland-Spingarn Research Center.*

Jet even called out African Americans for accepting white aesthetic inclinations and sneering at their continental kin. The magazine stated, "Because U.S. standards of beauty run to light skin, straight nose, thin lips and straight hair, American Negroes have often looked down upon their African cousins whose preferences in pulchritude often run to the opposite extreme."[53] The magazine continued by underscoring the global reach of white influence as it surfaced in the selection of Mercia Marshall as titleholder in the first national beauty contest held by South African natives. The report read, "But even African Zulus and Swazis are beginning to accept beauty standards of the white world." The "tea-colored" Swazi-Xhosa girl, according to the magazine, "might have run off with honors in beauty contests in any U.S. Negro community." In other words, Marshall represented a less purely African look and more of the nearly white or mulatto appearance so often seen as the beauty ideal elsewhere. The article even suggested that she was comparable to the last ten Miss Americas. Another line read, "Mercia never uses anything on her hair, except water, but a U.S. hairdresser would probably suggest other things for her." While sincere intentions to push for a more African-centered standard may have been present, *Jet* managed to demonstrate its own limits in appropriately discussing matters of ethnicity. The article passingly addressed African women as "Hottentots," a derogatory term coined by Dutch colonists and populations of the interior as "Africans in the jungle."[54]

While in some instances *Jet* magazine, in its coverage of Black beauty queens, seemed to rally against intraracial discrimination, it, too, was complicit in the phenomenon. Its 1953 "Most Beautiful Women in Negro Society" spread exalted "the gay, bejeweled, mink-coated circles which constitute the higher echelons on Negro society."[55] It branded all the women featured as "Negro belles." It named Grace Gladden of Washington, D.C., the "attractive olive-complexioned wife of orthopedic surgeon James Robert Gladden." About herself, she commented, "I've always been told I was good looking, but I've never paid any attention to it." Barbara Barland was voted one of Detroit's six most glamorous women and described as an exciting Detroit beauty "having coy, creole charm." The very next image proclaimed, "Mrs. Frances Parrish is a popular Louisville, KY society beauty whose looks are enhanced by her grey-green eyes. She is the wife of sociologist Dr. C.H. Parrish." Lois Lowe was called "a striking blond," and Kay Dixon, a former campus queen at Fisk, was marked a "Spanish type" Brooklyn beauty. The remarks blatantly connected lifestyle with status and beauty with color.

BEAUTIFUL NEGRO WOMEN

Grace Burroughs, Brooklyn, N.Y.; Dr. Mae McCarroll, New York and Mrs. Alfred Thomas, Detroit.

Also omitted were Ima Lou Pointer, Chicago, Janice Yates, Betti Mays, Marjul Cook, Sara Lou Harris, Sara E. Usher, Betty Jane Harmon, Charlotte Crump Poole, and Mrs. Marie Anderson (Sophie Tucker's maid).

More Beauties Next Month

Because of the overwhelming response received from our judges for this huge project, the editors of COLOR are forced to present a sequel to this compelling feature in our December issue. The latter issue of COLOR will contain the remaining fifty women who were not included this time due to the several reasons listed on Page 16. In addition, there will be many lovely ladies representing the southern and southwestern parts of the United States.

Thanks to the Judges

COLOR wishes to express sincere gratitude for the splendid cooperation shown by all of our judges (see Page 19 for pictures of judges), who sacrificed time from their daily work to assist in the monumental task of assembling "AMERICA'S 100 MOST BEAUTIFUL NEGRO WOMEN."

(Continued on next page)

MRS. ELEANOR DAILEY CYRUS, CHICAGO, ILLINOIS (above)—Mrs. Cyrus, the wife of Atty. Bindley C. Cyrus, a native of Bridgetown Barbados, B.W.I., is widely considered as the most beautiful Negro woman in the Chicago metropolitan area. She is the daughter of nationally prominent Dr. U. Grant Dailey.

Above: This headline in a 1949 issue of *Color*, a Black-owned publication, reads, "BEAUTIFUL NEGRO WOMEN." *Dr. Emory Tolbert/Popular Black Media Collection.*

Opposite: This woman with a crown is featured in a Queen Supreme hair dressing advertisement that promises to leave tresses "soft, lustrous and easy to fix." *Dr. Emory Tolbert/ Popular Black Media Collection.*

Sara Maddox, who eventually became Miss Alabama State University, grew up in 1950s Montgomery, Alabama, and remembered how complexion and pedigree impacted her formative years in the segregated city:

> *When I was running for Miss Booker T. Washington [High School] well I was a quiet person, kind of shy. In those days, though, you wouldn't have gotten elected any kind of homecoming queen, even in college, if you were fast, you know, or too popular in that sense of dating, they'd look for people who they thought were well rounded, but not out in the world. There were a group of students in the class above me that said, "We've gotten together for you to run for homecoming queen," and I said, "I don't*

You'll always be his sweetheart

...If you let lovely haircolor keep you young and beautiful

There's just no doubt he'll love you more if your hair shines and shimmers and feels soft against his cheek. Ask at your cosmetic counter for Godefroy's Larieuse Hair Coloring in the red box. Choose from 18 flattering colors.

Godefroy's **Larieuse**

GODEFROY MFG. CO. • 3510 OLIVE ST. • ST. LOUIS 3, MO.

The **QUEEN**
of them all...

Now with LANOLIN

QUEEN *Supreme*

Three generations of QUEEN users are thrilled with the new QUEEN Supreme—the pure white, light hair dressing that leaves hair soft, lustrous and easier to fix. 35¢, plus tax—at all good stores. Or send $1.00, plus tax—for three cans, from NEWBRO MANUFACTURING CO., Atlanta, Georgia.

want to do that." And when they finally talked me into it, I had to have petitions signed by all of the teachers in the school and they were attesting to my character. That was the purpose of that. There were two teachers, one became a good friend of mine later, but there were two teachers who said "Well honey, who are you, who are your people? Where do you live? Hmm…well come back and see me tomorrow." And I was just really hurt by that because most teachers said, "Oh, sure, OK." I knew a lot of them, most of them, but not all of them because it was a small school. And when I went back and reported to the student council, a sponsor, whose job was to oversee that, she got more upset than I did. And she gave those women a run for their money. These were Black women. They were fair skinned women. And I learned later, they didn't think I was an appropriate person to be running for homecoming because first of all, there was another girl that they thought was a better choice. And no one had nominated her. And she wasn't a smart girl, but she was a pretty girl. She had pretty long ponytails, curly ponytails. Not only that, but my family was just too poor, and [therefore] I was not invited to participate in the debutante ball. They [the women] said "Were you a deb?" I said, "No." "Well, honey, who are you?" Actually, after I graduated from college, I was elected to student teach at the white school because they were just integrating, these women came over there to work, we all worked together, the same two teachers of mine. But that was extremely hurtful; I'm almost crying now talking about it. I'm trying not to be a crybaby. But, I can remember that.[56]

Maddox suggested that African American children withheld certain information from their parents in efforts to not escalate existing burdens of working and raising a family in the Jim Crow South. She said, "You know I can't recall whether I took that home because a lot of things, you know, you wouldn't tell your parents. You just dealt with it." However, other school authorities and neighborhood adults acted as advocates for youth when and where they could. A woman in charge of the student election aided young Maddox in her dilemma.

The lady in charge, Frieda Burg. [You know how] in Color Purple the role Oprah played where she would walk as if she was marching? This lady was marching down the hall. She talked to this woman and when she came back she had signatures! She said, "Imagine them not signing a form because they think you should have more money or lighter skin or longer hair!" She said, "You go through life, don't let that alter your dreams."[57]

DO NEGROES PREFER LIGHTER WOMEN?

. . . . . AND LIGHTER MEN?

FRAT CROWNS A QUEEN—Lovely Lolo Boyd of Cheyney State Teachers College, ieyney, Pa., was crowned Mardi Gras Queen in Philadelphia by Omega Psi Phi frater- nity; but her popularity—not her color—determined her vic- tory. Pretty contestants of mixed colors are in background.

Omega Psi Phi fraternity's Mardi Gras Queen at Cheney State. *Chronicling America/Library of Congress.*

Maddox summarized her high school experience in pageantry saying, "Yes, in those days they wanted you to look a certain way."

Barbara Anders, a native of Tallahassee, Florida, and witness to intraracial beauty ideology conflicts, reiterated a similar point. Anders, Miss Senior Attendant 1959–60 at Florida A&M University, revealed how profound colorism was but how its grip started to loosen as she began her reign:

> *They didn't have many queens my color up until that time. It was only in the '60s that things began to change. They wanted someone who had the European kind of features and style.* [Interviewer asks, "Even at a Black school?"] *Especially at a Black school. That was the norm for beauty. Anglo beauty. As I look over the years, there were other dark*

attendants before me. And even they had a dark-skinned Miss FAMU. But typically it was someone who was light-skinned. Historically you thought of a queen as being the European type. Even boys who didn't marry girls who looked like that, would prefer that to be their queen. Not because they were against other looks, because they married those girls, but they just wanted to make sure that Florida A&M queen looked like that. That didn't bother us in the '60s because things were moving, changing. I was not a novelty, but I was not the norm either.[58]

Anders, like Maddox, remembered distinct moments in her childhood in which hue surfaced as a commonplace factor. She shared:

Skin color meant a lot, so by me being dark and the others were a little lighter, bothered me as a child. But I was still loved. I think my father's people were prejudiced along skin color lines. I think sometimes kids are sensitive to it, and I was because it made a difference in your mind how you were treated. My aunt was one of the persons....She would call me Black. And my mother told her, "Don't do that." To her it wasn't a term of endearment. I don't know why she did it. She was light skinned, as was my mother's mother....I was always considered a cute little Black girl. But it always had that adjective. [Laughter] *"For a Black girl, you're cute." But that still goes on today. Being Miss Senior by that time, it didn't stop me from doing anything.*[59]

She credited her loving mother and grandmother with preventing the verbal abuse from having a heavier or lasting impact on her personality or social skills, stating, "I dated around the clock, never had problems in that area. I was very popular in high school and college." Anders also said her mother's serious instructions to her aunt eventually stopped her from calling her "Black." From her perspective, modest living seems to have had little impact on how affluent African Americans interacted with the less well-to-do. She suggested that classism was less of an issue because of limited educational opportunities in Tallahassee for Blacks. She attributed the ultimate creation of an African American middle class to the establishment of historically Black colleges and universities (HBCUs). Without them, Anders said:

You were going to be in Tallahassee doing maid work or in Quincy picking tobacco. When HBCUs and FAMU opened up, people could go to college and become educated. And that is when the masses of people were able to go. That's when you get people who weren't necessarily offspring of the master. As things evolved and when integration came, everybody could go anywhere. That's why you see the Ivy Leagues always took Blacks. But they're selected Blacks, even some graduated in 1800s, but they were special people to have done that. But for the masses of people, the HBCUs are the reasons that they were able to get such massive education because it was provided for us.[60]

Anders described the Black community in Tallahassee as a tiny "fishbowl" where openings for separatism or exclusivity were few. "If you can picture it, Canal Street and Palm Meadow and Monroe and Adams were my life. My little circle. Dr. Fox's children and Dr. Foot's children lived in my neighborhood, and most [African American] doctors in Tallahassee lived in that area. I was friends with them and didn't see any real rejection from them."[61]

When Veronica Hicks Gibson (who later became Miss FAMU) became queen of the campus chapter of Kappa Alpha Phi fraternity and the Kappa Scrollers, their pledge group, the effects of colorism on how some young

Miss FAMU High with her attendants in the 1965 Florida A&M University homecoming parade heading west on Call Street in Tallahassee. *Florida Memory/State Library and Archives of Florida.*

Above: Florida A&M University homecoming queen Alberta Brown in the parade on Monroe Street in Tallahassee, October 16, 1965. *Florida Memory/State Library and Archives of Florida.*

Opposite, top: Florida A&M University's Miss Pre-Med in a convertible in 1965. *Florida Memory/State Library and Archives of Florida.*

Opposite, bottom: Gibbs Hall float in the FAMU homecoming parade on Monroe Street in Tallahassee, November 5, 1966. *Florida Memory/State Library and Archives of Florida.*

African American women saw themselves had not yet vanished. Gibson explained the anxiety that her responsibilities as queen exposed:

> *When they had to dress up I would march in front of them when they went to the auditorium or the cafeteria or basketball games. I would be the lead one, and it was good that there were only four or three that finished* [the pledging process], *but I was the lead person for them. Everybody would see me first and them behind me. And I was extremely nervous about that.*[62]

The apprehension about being in front, she revealed, stemmed from a hyperawareness of her color she had endured since she was a child, which was worsened when another young lady coarsely shared, "You're not the color that they normally have." Gibson stated that other students, too, underscored her title as the "Black" beauty. Upon becoming Miss FAMU her senior year, she recalled, "Right before my time there was no one darker than me besides Jackie Nixon."

Linda Grace Brown grew up in Monroeville, Alabama, and became Miss Union High School in 1964. She said she won her title because she was smart and popular, not because she was light skinned. She was a cheerleader with a star football player as her boyfriend. She did disclose, however, preferential treatment she received at other times as a result of her complexion:

> *They had junior majorettes, and they chose me and two others. And we all had long, straight hair. And we would practice but…we had no rhythm whatsoever. None. We were a disgrace to Black people.* [Laughs] *But anyway, I just went ahead and got out because I knew why I had been chosen. I had been chosen because I had the long, straight hair. I could not do the steps at all. I think that was one time my color and my hair, played a role.*[63]

While some experienced favoritism, others observed colorism from the opposite end. While attending ASU, Sara Maddox, Miss Alabama State 1968, still remembered a shopping incident decades after it occurred:

> *This is something that happened at college, and it speaks to the way that white people addressed Blacks based on their color. I had a classmate who looked white. I don't know that she was half white or one-fourth. But we were shopping in Montgomery Fair long ago, buying hosiery or something, and I was at the counter with Marion but we were together, and Marion said, "Let's move apart, see which one she is gonna wait on first." And the*

Sara Alice Martin (later Maddox) as Miss Alabama State University 1967–68. *Maddox family private collection.*

lady looked at her because she is fair [meaning light], *had the curly hair. "May I help you?" That was when Marion said, "Why don't you go first and let's see what she's going to do." So I approached the counter first, she was waiting on someone, and when she finished then Marion approached the counter and she says, "May I help you?" And I say, "Excuse me, I was first," and then she looked at Marion and then looked at me as if to say, "Is that all right?" and Marion said, "She was first," and the lady said, "OK." But you know, we experienced a lot of that, too. That was hurtful, because you knew if you were fair you got a little bit better treatment, if you were brown a little bit better, and people who had dark skin had it even worse, you know. Around maybe my senior year in high school I began to experience things that were really hurtful.*

Chapter 3

"THERE WAS A VIRTUAL EPIDEMIC OF NEGRO HOMECOMING QUEENS"

*Brewing Unrest and Pageants as Student Activism
in the Civil Rights Movement*

E arly childhood experiences of the young campus queens reveal the simultaneous feelings of contentment found within the tightknit community enjoyed at Black schools and the constant irritations of Jim Crow. Growing up in all-Black neighborhoods, for many, reinforced positive cultural values and a substantial measure of uniformity in socioeconomic and political identity. Still, growing up during segregation's unequal distribution of political freedom and job access produced lasting frustrations and a desire for justice in the world beyond their immediate surroundings. While the young women's time as student representatives brought fun, positive recognition and lessons in leadership, it could not fully shield them from racism that infiltrated the routine lives of all African Americans. Their memories bear witness to how color disrupted common play activities and academic pursuits. Yet the isolation from whites engendered freer spaces among themselves. Sara Maddox, of Montgomery, Alabama, remembered growing up near the school where she would eventually become queen:

> We lived in Patterson Court, very close to Alabama State. In Patterson, and everywhere in America, those were the days when you didn't have to worry about locking your doors. We were allowed to stay out after dark on our front lawn. We enjoyed hanging out with our friends. I mean right there on the porch, down the street, very close. When we were very young, we enjoyed playing jacks, hopscotch, trading comic books, playing ball and sometimes our neighbor would organize a talent show. We lived on a court

Griffin Junior High School queen and court in Tallahassee, Florida, in 1957. *Queen, in front seat*: Althemese Pemberton (later Barnes). *Driver*: Edwina Martin (later Bryant). *Back seat, left to right*: Pauline Houzell, Yvonne Cofield and Ida Mae Holloman. *Florida Memory/State Library and Archives of Florida.*

where there was a lawn. All the kids who lived in the circle or semicircle would stay out. That's where we had our talent shows. There came a time when that all changed. I can remember so well across the street from our apartment projects were rows of buildings. But just right across the street we can remember seeing the KKK going into the building for meetings. And I'm gonna say that might've been 1959, it could've been earlier. But when we saw them in the white, and I guess our parents must have seen them, everyone had to come inside. That was the end of our talent shows. We were not allowed to stay after dark. It didn't really have an impact on us as children because we really didn't know what was going on. Nobody discussed it with us. As we got older we were told, we learned things in school. Our grandmother in particular told us a little bit more.[64]

When Maddox got older, the once hazy racism that barely resonated as a child became clearer as interactions with whites were much more direct. The exchanges demonstrated that a great part of racial customs, particularly those upheld by whites not connected to legislation or law enforcement, grew

Miss Lincoln High School with her attendants in Tallahassee, Florida. Accompanying note: "Charming Ivella Landers, *center*, crowned Miss Lincoln High School for the '57–58 school year during colorful coronation ceremonies Tuesday evening, reigned during traditional homecoming festivities which began Tuesday and continued through Thursday. Her attendants are, *left*, Gloria Arnold and Delores Austin." *Florida Memory/State Library and Archives of Florida.*

out of tradition and emotional disturbance rather than any sensible logic. That said, some barriers were easier to break than others.

Senior high school, I remember this so well. We were seniors—had to do our first term paper, and we had all been given an author to research, and we had to read a novel by that author. I had to read something by William Makepeace Thackeray. I remember that very well. And one of my classmates who's a graduate of Talladega College, he was salutatorian at my high school and his wife a valedictorian, both went to Talladega. He and I, along with three or four other people, integrated the white library. In our library for the Blacks, which luckily was on our side of town, we just didn't find a lot of sources that we needed for our paper. He said, "Let's go to the white library." It was on the other side of town where I went to church. I believe it was in the Cleveland Avenue area, somewhere close to the YMCA maybe. I said, "I don't know, my grandmother won't like it if she knows I'm doing this." [He said,] "No, we're not making any trouble, we just want to get some information for our paper." We walked in, and the lady at the desk like sneered. And he was doing all the speaking. His name was Nathaniel Webb. Nathaniel took lead and said, "We don't want any trouble, we just need information so that we can get our term papers written." She said, "OK, but you will have to be quiet, and we don't want any troubles." She kept saying, "We don't want any troubles," and we said, "We don't want any trouble either, we just want to get our work done." I think maybe they thought Black men ought to be feared. I may be wrong, but I think he was the only boy. I think the rest of us were girls. Maybe one other. So to say "we don't want any trouble," that was just something they always thought that's what Black people were about. And I don't think they had to have a real basis for saying it, but just negative feelings for all of us most of the time. And we went there I think several times after that, working on the same paper, but then from that point on we could just go, but we never saw any other Black people there. You know, we just started spreading the word that it's OK, you can go in there. They will let you come in. So we give ourselves credit for having done that. [Smiles][65]

African Americans found other creative ways of satisfying their needs and interests. Mona Jackson, a future queen at Florida A&M, discussed her father's ingenuity in using his complexion to the benefit of his family. Although at one point she described her memories as "not too pleasant," Jackson emphatically insisted that segregation had not produced a sense of inferiority in terms of her self-esteem or academic pursuits:

I can remember being very young. We had segregated buses. They didn't want us to ride and mingle with the whites on the buses. They wanted us to ride in the back. However, my dad was very light in complexion. He would take us places, go in, get served and bring things to us, because they would serve him. But when they saw his little "pickaninnies" then they didn't want him to remain. I was small, and I just wondered about it and asked my dad about it. We talked about it, but he is not as much of an activist type, but he would get what he wanted for his kids. So if it meant he had to go to the Royal Castle and get what we needed, he would go in that way and do it. But my sister was older, and therefore she had an opportunity to participate in a lot of the marches, the Crandon Park [march] that was

[at] *Virginia Key Beach. She was involved with the students doing their swim-ins and things like that. At the time, the only place that Blacks could swim was Virginia Key Beach. And Crandon Park was the only place that the whites would swim in Miami. And therefore, in an effort to integrate it, they had students and civil rights activists here that did swim-ins at Crandon Park Beach. It didn't really bother me as much because I had grown up in a Black community. It was Richmond Heights. We had such a mixture of people living together. We had teachers, preachers, whatever. All living together, because a lot of Blacks could not own homes in other parts at the time, so I really grew up with a very good cross-section of role models, friends, and I grew up very secure, having a very good support base. I hear people saying, "It takes a village to raise a child," and I feel that during those times we had a great village. I can remember my elementary school principal attending my high school graduation. They followed us so well that we always had that support system. I remember in high school the books that were brought to us as new books were really books coming from Coral Gables Senior High, which was a white school close by. So when they were changing their books, we were getting them. And I think it might've been around tenth grade or ninth where they started introducing the new national science and math programs, then everyone was getting new books, even us. I think for me it made me stronger, made me want to really excel, made me realize that no matter what color or background, I could still achieve, and I found when I reached graduate programs, because I did go to Florida A&M, which was a Black school, but for my master's and my doctorate I went to school integrated. When I received my master's at Florida Atlantic there were times that I was the only Black in the class, and I felt wonderful because I could overachieve and over-excel. And all along we had been taught that we had the skills and we had excellent teachers who put time in with us. So I was very secure, whether I went to Florida A&M or Florida Atlantic or FIU, that I was going to be able to meet the challenge and do what I needed to do.*[66]

Veronica Hicks Gibson, who became Miss Florida A&M University, reiterated similar points about her upbringing in Miami. She said, "My class was extremely smart. I had a class of 127. So it was a very small school," with 2 salutatorians because they were all so academically competitive. Gibson stated that teachers from her school maintained a regular presence in the apartment complex where she lived, saying, "At that time teachers, doctors, an Indian chief, we all lived together, so there wasn't a stigma because it was segregated. Even though you're a doctor or a teacher, you couldn't move to other neighborhoods. You had to stay there."[67] She did, however, experience a stark contrast when leaving the utopia of her building to catch the bus to school. Like Jackson, she underscored its lack of impact on her interpretation of self. She shared the following about her elementary years:

You could feel it [discrimination on the bus]. *There was one lady in particular on the route that I took, and she was Caucasian or white and just extremely mean to African Americans. And it was almost understood that you go to the back of the bus. She enforced the law that you sat in the back of the bus. And she was very curt to African Americans. She was a huge white lady. Big shoulders and stuff, really masculine. And she enforced her persona. Her persona represented what she was in essence. I remember so much being on the bus and sitting at the back of the bus, that we passed one elementary school, which is Sunset Elementary school over here. And I would notice their textbooks in compare to my textbooks, which were battered and worn, and they had brand-new books. And we of course right over here, right off of 62nd, we got the used books at that time. Things were the same in high school, as for textbooks, but the kind of teachers we had in that time instilled in you that you could, because we were very close to Coral Gables High* [for whites]. *This was one of the top ten schools in the nation. Top ten in the nation! And they always said that you have to do twice as good to be equal to them. And you had to work twice as hard. But they never said you couldn't do it. And I didn't feel less than, but I knew that I was being treated less than. And that was…I don't know how you can express it…it was to the point that you expected to respect the laws that were in order and what was law at the time. So I had to abide by them. But my mom raised me to believe that I can do and be anything I want to. And it was just she and I when, you know, if we were to buy a kit to make a cabinet, or the lights or something, a lamp would go out, she'd say, "Well, there are instructions, Ronnie (and that's my nickname), we can do it." And that's why you're going to school, so that you can learn and you follow these things. And nobody was ever better than me.*[68]

Barbara Anders, another FAMU queen from Tallahassee, Florida, concurred. She, in fact, suggested that many African Americans in her community remained fairly unconcerned with integration efforts because they perceived themselves as progressive without white proximity. She said, "Because we were so isolated, we didn't care if we integrated or not, because

The marching band in the Florida A&M University homecoming parade heading west on Call Street in Tallahassee in 1965. *Florida Memory/State Library and Archives of Florida.*

we thought that we were just as good or better than the people we saw downtown who were discriminating against us. We thought we had a very, very good life. We used secondhand band uniforms [in high school]; the Marching 100 would give FAMU High its old band uniforms. We got old instruments. We got beat-up stuff, not from the white folks like they did in the rural country. We got stuff from the college. All our textbooks as far as I know were new."[69]

Linda Brown, 1964's Miss Union High, told a similar story about growing up in Alabama. She remembered parents of African Americans engaging in strategic actions to protect their children "from being intimidated by white folk or being snubbed by white folk." She said, "One of my friends said when they'd go on trips they'd pack lunches for days, and her parents would say, 'Oh, we're going on this big picnic and stop at this park'..." The parents made their stops fun to disguise the fact that they could not rest or dine at most hotels or restaurants. "Of course they didn't serve Negros." Brown also remembered receiving hand-me-down clothes from "Sissy," a young white girl for whose family Brown's mother cleaned. "They were owners of the sawmill in Monroeville, I think, so they were well-to-do." About the clothes, Brown asserted, "They were brand-new to me! And they looked better than

Southwest Elementary School girls in the play *The Season of Happiness* in Tallahassee, Florida, in 1960. Patricia Ann Haynes is crowned queen of the seasons during the presentation of the three-act operetta. *Florida Memory/State Library and Archives of Florida.*

anybody else's, so what was I to complain about!" These firsthand accounts challenge other civil rights–era narratives that suggest most Black people felt inferior as a result of segregation. "They [Caucasians] were just a different breed of people. We weren't jealous of what they had or anything. No."

Several of the queens expressed their own hesitation or their families' reluctance to become directly active in the civil rights movement. Perhaps the sense of comfort they felt in their communities diminished any immediate need they saw for something different. Others, however, avoided involvement because they feared job loss or reprisals that might have further complicated their already difficult lives for African Americans living under national apartheid. Barbara Anders expressed regret at having not committed to activism on campus the way she saw her peers participate. She was good friends with Patricia Due, who was arrested with nine other FAMU students for attempting to order at a white-only Woolworth lunch counter in 1960. In a demonstration several days later, Due was teargassed in the face by police and suffered permanent eye damage. The incident garnered nationwide attention by way of support from Martin Luther King Jr. and Jackie Robinson. Anders reflected:

> *I hope I can say this without crying. 1954—I was still in high school.* Brown v. Board of Education. *But I was in college at FAM when the young lady who is Patricia Due, who lives in Quincy now, was on campus. She and several other students did the sit-in demonstrations. I think I could've been a part of them because they were going on before I left the internship, but because my mother was a teacher in Leon County we were told not to get involved. Cause your parents' livelihood could be threatened if you were caught. So most people in Tallahassee didn't participate. The Steele boys (Reverend C.K. Steele's sons)—that was an exception. Their father was the president of the NAACP. For the most part, we were too chicken to know the significance of what was happening. And we didn't go to jail because we were afraid that it would jeopardize our parents. I didn't participate. When Patricia Due, my friend, and I talk about the movement, I say, "Pat, I'm sorry that I was not more conscious of what was happening." She says, "Don't worry, everybody gets to help in a different way." Tries to make me feel better, but I never feel better about the fact that I was in college during this turbulent time and I just sat there and it passed me by. Patricia Due stayed in jail for fifty days. She could've gotten out but refused to post the bond. She wanted to make a statement by staying in jail. She's written up in all the books for student movements.*

Arizona Tribune

TRUTH · JUSTICE · LIBERTY · EQUALITY

FIFTH YEAR, NO. 17
FRIDAY, NOV. 9, 1962

Pictorial Weekly

PHOENIX 49, ARIZONA
BR. 5-8391 TEN CENTS

ALPHA KAPPA ALPHA SORORITY PLANS FOR REGIONAL CONFERENCE

A planning session of the conference committee of the Alpha Kappa Alpha sorority, Delta Beta Omega chapter, washeld Thursday in the Maricopa Room of the Hotel Adams.

Seated are Miss Veros Johnson, registration chairman; Mrs. Charles Moten, Mrs. R. B. Phillips, general conference chairman; Mrs. M. Alice Marlott, hostficus; and Mrs. A. D. Hart.

Standing are Mesdames William Corbin, Ann Taylor, William Owens, and Jimmie Brooks.

Mrs. Will James another member is not shown.

The regional conference of the sorority is scheduled in the city next summer. Four states including Arizona, California, Oregon and Washington will be represented.

MISS HAZEL ECHOLES CHOSEN HOMECOMING QUEEN AT PUHS

Miss Dorothy Echoles, 19 yr. old Phoenix College student, congratulates her sister, Miss Hazel Echoles, 16 yr. old Phoenix Union High School senior who was selected as the homecoming queen. Miss Hazel Echoles is majoring in college preparatory. Her favorite subjects are economics, history and government.

An extremely active person, she is the president of the Jr. Sophiaritions, and a member of the junior choir of First Institutional Baptist Church.

She won the Phoenix Union High School junior citizenship award sponsored by the Phoenix Jr. Chamber of Commerce.

She is a member of the Girls League and a staff member of the school newspaper.

Her ambition is in the field of medicine. She hopes to be a physical therapist.

She is participating in the on the job training program at the office of Dr. Oscar A. Hardin, 1 N. 12 Street.

The sisters are the daughters of Mr. and Mrs. Edward Echoles, 1605 E. Madison St.

DOROTHY DANDRIDGE FILES FOR HER DIVORCE

LOS ANGELES--Actress Dorothy Dandridge filed suit to divorce Jack Denison, her husband of three years.

Miss Dandridge charged cruelty and mental suffering in the Superior Court suit.

The actress was nominated for an Academy award as best actress for the picture "Carmen Jones" in 1956.

Miss Dandridge also appeared in the picture "Porgy and Bess."

MAYOR PROCLAIMS EQUAL OPPORTUNITY WEEK IN THE CITY

Mayor Sam Mardian has proclaimed Monday, November 19, as Equal Opportunity Day, as part of the nationwide observance sponsored by the National Urban League.

The Phoenix Urban League sponsors of the event, which marks the 99th anniversary of President Lincoln's Gettysburg Address. It is the seventh such observance of the Urban League. This date was chosen for the occasion because of Lincoln's concern as expressed in his first message to the Congress, that "All have an unfettered start and a fair chance in the race of life." Mayor Mardian asks every citizen to "do everything in his power to advance this cause so that all Americans will understand and appreciate the great advantages of our democratic way of life."

William Roselius, industrial relations manager of the Sperry Phoenix Company, is chairman of this special day.

The Phoenix Urban League is an organization devoted to improving opportunities for Negroes and bettering race relations in Phoenix. It is an affiliate of the National Urban League and a member agency of the Phoenix United Fund.

NOV. 11 IS NAACP SUNDAY

LOS ANGELES -- The subregional office of the National Association for the Advancement of Colored People announced Sunday, November 11 has been proclaimed "NAACP Day".

The proclamation signed by Acting Mayor Harold A. Henry pursuant to a directive from Mayor Sam Yorty, who is away from the city, urges all Los Angeles citizens to join in doing everything possible to assure the success of the day's activities in fund raising.

Medger W. Evers, Mississippi NAACP Field Secretary, will be the principal speaker at the "Mississippi Rally" to be held at the New Hope Baptist Church at 3:00 p.m., November 11.

The "Mississippi" Rally is sponsored by the Sub-Regional Office, NAACP, the Baptist Ministers Conference of Los Angeles, NAACP, the Broadway Federal Savings and Loan, Golden State Mutual Life Insurance Company and numerous individuals.

SOLDIER–SCIENTIST–INVENTOR WINS THE OMEGA MAN OF THE YEAR

Sgt. First Class Adolphus Samms, a soldier scientist stationed at Yuma Test Station, will receive the Omega Psi Phi fraternity "Man of the Year" award, Sunday, Nov. 11.

A special program is scheduled at Phillips CME Church, 1601 E. Adams at 10 a.m. Mr. William McClellan will present the main address titled, "Automation, A Challenge of the Future."

Sgt. Samms recently received a patent on his frame center support invention that could eliminate engines in the second and third stages of multi-stage rockets. His invention introduces a new concept in rocket development and it would save money. He explains his invention and its applications in treatise "Advanced Design Rocket Boosters."

Stationed at Yuma, Arizona for the past four years, Sgt. Samms is a native of Boston where he attended grammar school and Boston Trade High School.

He obtained no further formal education after his trade school work, but he educated himself in science through extensive reading and experiments.

His latest patent is the fourth he has received on space age inventions. He has seven others pending.

The 39 year old soldier has been in service for nearly twenty years. He may retire next year and enter the field of missile research.

MRS. MILLER HONORED AT FAREWELL PARTY ON WESTSIDE

A group of relatives and friends bade a Phoenician farewell last Saturday night.

Shown above are Mesdames Bertha Jackson, Urbana Miller, Evelyn Hopper, Esther Ford, Evelyn Chambers, Sylvia Thompson, and Amelia Turner.

Mrs. Miller, honoree, leaves by jet on Nov. 10, to join her husband T/Sgt. Robert L. Miller, who is stationed in Bitburg, Germany. She will be accompanied by her three children.

A farewell party was held at the home of Mr. and Mrs. William Thompson, 1405 S. 18 Avenue.

ELLINGTON TO BE AT RAMADA INN SOON

acclaimed throughout the world as the creator of a new, rich and distinctly American musical idiom.

In January, 1943, the Duke played his first concert at New York's Carnegie Hall. At that time he introduced his first great and ambitious work, "Black, Brown and Beige," a "Tone Parallel To The History of the Negro in America."

Since that first concert he has played concerts in Cleveland, Boston, Philadelphia, Los Angeles, Chicago and other key cities, always to capacity houses. The Duke is currently in the midst of one of his most triumphant concert tours. He recently took time out to appear on the Edie Adams and Tonite television shows.

Don't miss this rare opportunity to hear "America's Genius of Modern Music."

Duke Ellington and his famous orchestra will present a concert at the Ramada Inn, November 16 8:30 p.m.

Featuring his well-known and brilliant soloists, Johnny Hodges, Harry Carney, Ray Nance, and Milt Grayson, the Duke's program will range from the semi-classic to jazz, "Black and Tan Fantasy" and "Jam with Sam."

Critics say Duke Ellington's music and Walt Disney's cartoons are the only two original art forms America has produced. True or not, Ellington is

Tickets are on sale at the Century Skyroom, 1121 E. Washington, and at Sandy's Record Shop, at 43 E. Monroe. Admission is $4.00 and $3.50.

Miss Phoenix Union High announced in the November 9, 1962 *Arizona Tribune*. *Chronicling America/Library of Congress.*

Miss Florida A&M University, Diane Spratling (later Bargman), dancing at a ball with escort Herbert Smith, October 1, 1967. *Florida Memory/State Library and Archives of Florida.*

Tallahassee kids were very involved. Some professors would try to make you not, and you had other professors saying, "Go for it!" Even helping get you out of jail. They were afraid for the students, and then they didn't want to upset the status quo.[70]

Diane Bargman, Miss FAMU 1968, also had parents concerned about any involvement with political activism. She recalled her mother's and father's inquiries when they learned the Student Non-Violent Coordinating Committee's (SNCC) national head, Stokely Carmichael, had visited the university in April 1967. "I remember my parents saying, 'Did I see you in there?' I said, 'No I was on campus in the triangle, you didn't see me there.'"[71] She also noted the transition from articulations of the struggle for civil rights being rooted in moral suasion to more forceful vocalizations grounded in a demand for liberation.

Bargman said the campus was headed into "the Black Power kind of thing." She, like Anders, adhered to her parents' warnings, saying, "I kind

Miss FAMU Diane Spratling (later Bargman) sports leather gloves while escorted by Herbert Smith, October 14, 1967. *Florida Memory/State Library and Archives of Florida.*

of stayed to myself. I was quiet. So I really didn't get out to really what was going on." She repeated that although she herself was not involved, student activism and interest was at its peak. "You did have a movement of Black Power. It made you more appreciative of those people that really fought to try to bring forth civil rights."[72]

The larger student population held a growing dissatisfaction with the 1960s' slow pace of response and enforcement of those legal victories promised in the 1950s. This was exacerbated at Florida A&M University when white lawmakers and officials powered the demise of the FAMU hospital and law school, in addition to reallocating those resources to Florida State University

Miss Tuskegee Institute Brenda Dickerson and her court raise their fists, reflecting the political mood of the era. Photographed in 1970. *Archives at Tuskegee University.*

just down the hill. Moreover, a looming threat of a merger of the two only swelled the tension. Professor Glenda Alice Rabby, scholar on civil rights in Tallahassee, wrote, "Student opinion about the merger was overwhelmingly negative."[73] Roscoe Ellis, a student leader on campus, summarized the sentiment when he told a *Florida Flambeau* reporter that "students would burn down every building on this campus" before they would allow a merger with a white institution. Veronica Hicks Gibson also recalled Carmichael's visit to campus and the overwhelming response to his call to action:

> *Stokely Carmichael came and drove up in a station wagon. And he said, "You're either in or you're out. You're either in the movement or out of the movement. And you need to stand up." He said, "I'm supposed to be over at FSU." That's the one he came to speak to. But he came to the Black school. And then he said, this is in one of our yearbooks, "I'm standing here on a car speaking to all of you and—and your auditorium was right here—why can't I speak to you in an assembly?"* [referencing campus administrators who had not approved his visit] *And someone ran over, jumped up on the building went up on the second floor, came back*

*down and opened up the doors and everybody ran in. He was not scheduled
to come to FAM. He was scheduled to speak at FSU. He just happened
to....I don't know why he decided, but for some unknown reason before it
was over, that auditorium was jam-packed.*[74]

Gibson, from Miami, frustratingly remembered moving to Tallahassee for
college, saying, "When I went to FAM, I saw the most prejudiced people
that I've ever seen in my life. 'Cause Tallahassee is the capital, so…when we
went downtown they would not let you try your shoes or your hat without
tissue paper. They talked down to us. I absolutely hated Tallahassee."[75]
However, what fueled African Americans' increasingly aggressive stance was
rooted not in water fountain assignments and bathroom door signs but the
hardened restrictions to political participation, higher levels of education,
employment and pay, and thus, a total barricade to both upward mobility
and full equality in America. African Americans recognized 1863 and the
surrounding years as the end of legalized slavery. Therefore, their present
reflections on one hundred years of progress, or a lack thereof, served
as a sharp reminder of the United States' outright refusal to extend full
citizenship to African Americans regardless of what methods they used to
bargain for it. While Gibson summarized her feelings with "In Tallahassee,
it was absolutely the most horrific experiences I've had," Barbara Anders
explained what job options looked like even by the 1960s:

*One of the things that I remember about the year they did the demonstrations
and the sit-ins, I was interning in Miami. I was in theater, and you had
to do internships to graduate. I was a theater major but English minor.
In order to teach, I had to do an internship. What am I gonna do in the
'60s other than teach? If I'm not a nursing student or whatever? The
significance of that is that job opportunities in the South, there were no
factory jobs like in the North. You could either be a domestic or, if you had
an education, you could be a teacher. That was the bulk of what Black
people who finished college did. The ones who had the aptitude could go on
to become doctors and nurses, but there was really not an accredited nursing
school that people could go to right out of high school until the '60s. So if
you wanted to be a nurse, first you go to Tuskegee, couple of other HBCUs.
This is in my lifetime. If I wanted to be a doctor, I would have to leave
the state of Florida. That is pure and simple up until maybe years after
I finished from college that the other institutions in Florida and Miami
opened up their medical schools. If you wanted to be an accountant, there*

Left: Close-up view of a Florida A&M University homecoming parade float on Monroe Street in Tallahassee. Accompanying note: "The day's activities started at 10 a.m. with a big parade which wound through Tallahassee streets from the Benjamin-Banneker Building on the campus to Brevard street where it disbanded." October 16, 1965. *Florida Memory/State Library and Archives of Florida.*

Below: Vocational Tech float on Monroe Street in Tallahassee, Florida, October 16, 1965. *Florida Memory/State Library and Archives of Florida.*

Miss ROTC float in the FAMU homecoming parade on Monroe Street in Tallahassee, November 5, 1966. *Florida Memory/State Library and Archives of Florida.*

was no MBA. The majors in colleges were limited. Howard U was the capstone for Black people who wanted to go into professions. We had no law school at FAMU then, not from '56 to '60. No, I correct myself, FAMU law school was there....I could have gone. They opened it in the '50s, so I was still in high school. But the bulk of people who finished had to go into teaching. That's how I knew I wasn't gonna be an actress; I knew there would be no roles for me in Tallahassee. If I had gone to New York at that time, even now there are limited roles. So I didn't disillusion myself that I was gonna be a star on Broadway or the motion pictures. I always wanted to be in children's theater. That's what I ended up trying to do.[76]

Veronica Hicks Gibson remembered the vow she made to herself upon witnessing her mother relegated to one of the few fields of work Anders mentioned, domestic service.

My mother made thirty dollars a week. I pledged to myself at that time that I would never work on a job for anyone as a domestic. I would never have people come to my door for insurance. I don't know if you have witnessed this. They call you Alice [by first name], and you call them Mr. Charley [by last name]. I said it would never happen. For the newspaper, they would come to your door and you had to call them Mister! And they called you Alice! I pledged to myself, I made a vow to me, "Ronnie, you will never have anyone knock on your door to collect anything." Almost in my whole complex, they were maids. And even when we moved to the Grove. I moved to a three-story apartment complex, almost all of the mothers were domestics. Now, we did have a teacher, we had a guy that worked for the county, we had a numbers runner [laughter], we had...most of the fathers worked construction, they go to work, clean, they come back dirty, dusty. But most of the mothers there, they were domestics. Also, at that time thirty dollars a week was a really small amount of money. And sometimes my mom could not meet all of her obligations. And she would say to me, "Go to her door, tell them I'm not home." And I vowed to myself, I would never go through that in my life.[77]

Meanwhile, Sara Maddox observed the commotion on Alabama State University's campus in Montgomery, the principal seat of the civil rights movement. She described her freshman year, 1964–65, as "tumultuous." She remembered the Southern Christian Leadership Conference (SCLC) and the Black Panther Party maintaining a presence around the city but noted, "On our campus there were always representatives of the Student Non-Violent Coordinating Committee." She continued:

You could walk along campus any time and you might see a group together, and they're held spellbound by some speaker who's encouraging them to participate and get involved; they were really pulling students. I had a friend who left college to go off and for a year left school and went on the road with SNCC. And he did come back, did graduate, and he was a principal in DeKalb County. Clarence Montgomery. He is a retired principal. Once we had a big sit-in on campus, and there were so many students, the entire Hall Street was blocked off. Somebody called the police, and next thing I know I see police on horses, swinging their billy clubs, hitting people on the

Left: Miss Florida A&M University Jacqueline Nickson (later Cotman) with her mother in 1966. *Cotman family private collection.*

Right: Miss Florida A&M University Jacqueline Nickson poses for festivities in a mink stole. *Cotman family private collection.*

head, knocking them out. And the next thing here's a paddy wagon. I had never seen that before. They jump out, open doors, push students in, and I felt like I was on the outskirts because I was not right in the center of the street where they were getting people. I felt like my life was spared. I was not hit in the head or didn't have a horse trample over my feet because I was on the sidewalk. But those people on the street, a lot of them got hurt. They would just march in with the horses and trample over people.[78]

Maddox recalled certain demonstration being about the Vietnam War. She noted Black students' particular concern about being drafted because they lacked the financial capacity to avoid being recruited. "If students' grades were not a certain GPA, they could get drafted. That was the center of most of the unrest." She discussed the significance of all the local historically Black colleges collaborating on the issue, saying, "I can say that ASU, Alabama A&M and Tuskegee, all those students were interacting together because they didn't feel that it was fair for Blacks in the first place to go to Vietnam when we didn't even have equal rights here in our own country. So you can understand the anger." Additionally, she said, "Most Blacks didn't have parents who could send them off to another country, to Canada. Because we were told that people were able to escape across the borders to escape like President Clinton. To escape being drafted." Maddox lamented the sense of loss the war brought to the campus and community. "During that year," she offered, "because during the war there were so many funerals, so many young men killed, so many…it just seemed like every month there was a funeral."[79]

As college students rejected the status quo, one of their primary objectives would be to contest image-based oppression—specifically for women. Just as the aforementioned queens acknowledged the shift toward a more political mood on their own campuses, the trend struck elsewhere. Students staged demonstrations that specifically dealt with the issue of beauty, among others. These events challenged conventional notions of beauty and helped to crystallize racial identity and solidarity among African Americans on both white and HBCU campuses within the context of the era's national turmoil and mass protests.

At the decade's opening, Annette Jones White personified the fusion of queenship and student activism. Initially anxious upon entering Albany State College (University now), another historically Black college, she credited her growth as an outspoken student leader to modeling herself after Barbara Sanchez, a Miss Albany State, who White said "was just great" and very involved.[80] "Because my freshman year the Alphas picked me to be Miss Alpha—that did a great deal for my self-confidence." She added, "I mean, there were a lot of girls on campus who were pretty and, to me, sophisticated, and I just seemed like a little bumpkin from Corn Street! Corn [really is the name of] my street! Every time I'd say it, they'd laugh [laughter]. So that did a lot to help."[81] As her self-assuredness and assertiveness heightened and she became more reflective on some of her most painful interactions with Jim Crow, her impulse to incite change surged. She recalled her earliest memories of racial inequality:

> *When I was five, Santa Claus had refused to talk to me, reaching around me to grab the white children instead. Even as a little girl, the harsh realities of racism and segregation were readily apparent to me. I also remembered the time I was shopping downtown as a teenager. I tried to enter the last store on my list with my arms full of packages. As I entered, a white man slammed the door in my face, leaving me to walk home, humiliated, with a bloody nose.*[82]

Such memories coupled with newfound confidence formed White's conviction to exercise change by working as a student agent for the local NAACP Youth Council and waking up "at the crack of dawn" to sweep, type, facilitate training sessions or perform any chores that met the organizational needs of the Albany arm of SNCC. Alongside White and other Albany State students who later became major civil rights figures, Dr. Bernice Johnson Reagon organized the Grammy-winning Sweet Honey in the Rock women's vocal ensemble and steered many of the foundational events that would ultimately become known as the Albany Movement. Martin Luther King Jr. supported the group in December 1961. In the spring of 1961, White ran for and won Miss Albany State—a position made attractive because it offered a full scholarship. Her father endured difficulties covering her tuition and often did carpentry work for staff and faculty at the school to subsidize her education.

White and just a few others launched a sit-in at the whites-only Artic Bear Restaurant and canvassed the Albany State dorms to recruit trial protesters in support of those who had been arrested in an earlier bus terminal demonstration. They marched on city hall, and she was among forty women taken outside of Albany to Newton, Georgia, and jailed. Albany State's administration, under extreme pressure from local and state authorities and terrorizations from white supremacists, threatened her position and the coming coronation if she continued an affiliation with the movement. She was, however, given a coronation during which the college's president, William H. Dennis, dropped, rather than placed, the crown on her head. His actions reflected his frustrations about job loss concerns and negative media frenzy as a result of Black student activism. Soon after, in response to White's participation at city hall, President Dennis suspended her and stripped her of her crown and its accompanying scholarship. Eventually, she was completely expelled.

Globally, the 1960s were marked by young people demanding change. A year after Annette White's march on city hall, South African government officials arrested and imprisoned Nelson Mandela in 1962 for stirring a workers' strike—one in a long chain of events that would solidify his leading role in dismantling apartheid. James Meredith officially enrolled at the University of Mississippi, thereby integrating the school in a state with a deadly history of lynching Black men and forced sterilization of Black women. His safety required the presence of U.S. federal marshals ordered by Attorney General Robert Kennedy to escort him. Despite the chaos elsewhere, student Robin Gregory described her initial experiences at

Howard University that year as uneventful. She said it held a tempered public posture curated by a conservative administration, comparable to the one at Albany that instigated Annette Jones White's expulsion. She also described its highly gendered expectations of students promoted within the culture of respectability. Specifically, she pointed to Howard's administration and its policies for women:

> *Like, one of the things that first happened when we went there was that all the women had a special assembly. And we were brought in, Patricia Harris was the dean of women at that time, and we had this lecture on etiquette, you know, and how we were supposed to dress and how we were supposed to behave. And you know, we were supposed to be ladies, and I didn't quite, you know, accept that for myself, and I didn't feel like I had to conform to that sort of thing either, because I didn't live on the campus. I lived in Washington, D.C.*[83]

The campus conservatism, and perhaps even general political inactivity among students, permeated into some of their social dispositions and interactions. Gregory labeled many as "middle class" and wanting "to have a good time." She shared that there was a "lack of deep thinking," and many young women sought out marriage as an ultimate objective. Moreover, many African Americans beyond Howard adhered to canons of appearance and conduct heavily influenced by white America and its wield of power. Western standards, because of their deep roots in national identity, in addition to the reinforcement of global racism, impacted average African Americans who sought to rid themselves as much as possible from the negative presumptions that prevalent associations with unfavorable images generated. A 1962 *Negro Digest* article put it succinctly: "All of these myths have economic reasons for being and they support an economic arrangement of which we are a part."[84] Sara Maddox, Miss ASU, said, "Those were the same days when people who wore afros—well, you better cut it off if you want to get a job and keep a job. I know people who have gotten into trouble at work not because of something they said but because of the way they carry themselves." Some African Americans, then, seeking safety, acceptance, achievement, fair housing and financial upward mobility, followed, as best they could, standards set by the dictating establishments that controlled access to these aspirations.

Hair certainly factored heavily as a perceived conduit to measuring acceptability. African American straightened styles, achieved through chemicals or heat, were so customary that many were alarmed by another's deviation. Gregory's unpopular decision to wear her hair naturally, which formed an afro, met initial resistance. She resolved to wear it in its natural state in 1964 after working with the Student Non-Violent Coordinating Committee in Washington, D.C., as a liaison to the Mississippi office. SNCC was seen as the younger and more militant answer to Dr. Martin Luther King's Southern Christian Leadership Conference. People would call from Mississippi to chronicle some of the violent incidents occurring there so that she could inform the office of Nicholas Katzenbach, the attorney general, and report it. That summer, Gregory attended the 1964 Democratic Convention in Atlantic City, during which the Mississippi Freedom Democratic Party ran eminent civil rights revolutionary Fanny Lou Hamer as its delegate. Gregory said some of the women who came from the South were wearing their hair naturally, and she decided to do the same after interpreting the style as an affirmation of heritage. However, she revealed that responses were "pretty negative."

> *You know, well, I came back home, and I was wearing my hair like that, and my family was pretty horrified. I got a lot of comments from people on the street. You know, people got angry about it. It was like I was exposing a secret. That was the first reaction. That reaction went on a long time because I didn't have a lot of company. You know, there weren't other people doing it. Maybe one or two other people were doing it. Well, there was one person in particular who had worn her hair like that for a year prior to that, or maybe even two, and that was Mary Lovelace, who was Stokely Carmichael's girlfriend at the time. So, you know, there was no precedent before that. But the response was pretty negative.*[85]

Within two years, the political climate at Howard, like that around the nation, had shifted. By 1966, the diplomatic tone of the civil rights movement had waned, while the stern tenor of Black consciousness heightened. Students rallied to articulate more boldly their political philosophies for African American progress and core Black aesthetic values. Gregory's election as homecoming queen evidenced the student movement. She recalled:

> *Someone came up with an idea that we should make a statement around the homecoming, because it was such a superficial kind of thing that kept affirming, um, old values that we were trying to resist or trying to overthrow. So I was approached by some men from the law school, and*

they asked me if I would do it, because they wanted to make a statement about the Black aesthetic. And they wanted to resist the whole image. This whole homecoming queen thing was, it's kind of hard to describe the atmosphere the way that it went, but it was a lot of fraternities, you know, the fraternities would nominate a candidate who would run for the position. And it was a popular election, by the way. But you had to be nominated by some on-campus organization. And usually they picked someone who was as close to white as they could possibly get. I mean, it didn't have to be skin color. It was just the, the whole image of the person. And so they said, "Well, will you do this? We want to run somebody that has a natural hairstyle. We know that you're politically active. Let's take this particular context and use it to make a statement." And so I was willing to do that. That's how it happened.[86]

Interestingly, the "whole image" concept Gregory mentioned appeared to have influenced how *Jet* reported her historic campaign for centennial homecoming queen. Although Gregory had a honey hue, the magazine announced, "Dark Girl 100th Anniversary Homecoming Queen."[87] Her afro or political leanings and campus activities, certainly not her skin color, must have inclined the writer to designate her as "dark" and "black" throughout the article. Gregory discussed her campaign strategy to "put as many Black images out as possible." Her printed materials featured African American men and women who were wearing natural hairstyles confidently. *Jet* reported, "Throughout the week Robin's sponsors presented her in positive ways to demonstrate Black beauty and Black pride. One day she arrived at campaign time in a Sting Ray. Each day her supporters carried 18x20 photos of her in attractive poses." The night of the pageant, she performed a silent drama featuring modern dance that captured the African presence in America from slavery into the future in the age of "computers." "Finally, after a blackout, Robin appeared in a lovely ball gown and afro hairstyle. The applause was tremendous."[88]

She shared, however, that her fellow candidates either could not or would not take her seriously. "They were real irritated by the fact that I was making it a political campaign." Hence, the night of the formal competition, upon the announcement of Gregory as the winner, "all the other women were really shocked. They just were flabbergasted." Howard's long administrative history and culture of steering clear of perceived radicalism manifested in the reactions of the other women. "They couldn't accept, you know, that someone looking like I was looking, right? I mean,

Robin Gregory's coronation in 1967. *Moorland-Spingarn Research Center.*

the way you're looking at me now, I mean, you can't perceive it. And, and they were just stunned." She described the crowd and the meaning of the moment that evening:

> *So when I went out there was pandemonium in the auditorium. I mean, people were screaming and jumping up and down and just sort of going nuts, you know. And there is a photograph, you know, I think I had my mouth wide open, you know? Sort of a high moment. It was very important in terms of self-acceptance. It seems superficial in a sense because it's an appearance thing. But for anybody who lived through that, there were years of self-denial and abnegation, you know, and nonacceptance of the way that Black people looked to themselves because of media images, and there was a lot of shame. You know, the reason why people were so angry with me was because I was coming out in public in a way that I shouldn't have been revealing myself, you know? It was like this secret, you know? You're not supposed to show that you have nappy hair, or something. So it was a really dramatic moment.*[89]

Still, Howard's administration was much less enthusiastic than the student audience on the night she won. It hesitated to honor her with the grandeur usually awarded to campus queens. For instance, Gregory did not receive the annual queen's reception normally hosted by the university. Furthermore, she divulged, "There was supposed to be a float that the students put together for the homecoming queen, and they didn't want to do it. I had to get some other people to do it for me. So there was a lot of snubbing going on." However, much like earlier high points in the civil rights movement, media attention altered the course of acceptance. Gregory also noted:

> When the media began to report this stuff, people were really turned on by it. A lot of men wrote to me from prison. They were really excited about what I was doing. You know, they were saying things like "This is—I've been waiting for something like this. For a sister to come out, and just be her natural self, and to say that we are beautiful as a people." So I got a lot of positive feedback from prisoners. Male prisoners. I got some marriage proposals! It was interesting, because then people began to focus on other things—the things we really wanted them to focus on. And you sort of have to do a thing like this to get people to look at other issues on the campus.[90]

Her election helped to spawn other political protests with national and international implications. General Lewis B. Hershey, head of the military draft board, had been invited to Howard University but met serious objection from the student population, given the general awareness about the disproportionate number of African American men being sent to the Vietnam War—an already highly contested global conflict. When students understood that he was invited to speak, they decided to stage a demonstration. Gregory asserted, "In essence, we didn't allow him to speak. There was a lot of shouting from the audience. There was a number of people that had placards that stormed the stage and just booed him, essentially, out of the auditorium."[91] She recalled Howard's predicament as a recipient of federal funding and other formal and informal ties to the government. She stated, "I think it has to be realized that Howard University was run like a plantation. Washington, D.C., could not vote. The people of Washington, D.C., could not vote. It was run by a southern committee of, of southern senators called the District Committee." She held southern white racist senators, as well as General Hershey, responsible for controlling the administration and student activities. As a result, students intentionally disrupted his visit to the university. Students shouted insults throughout his presentation. "One of them was 'beast,' and people sort of loved that word, and so they were shouting that. And every time he would try to speak, someone would say that." At one point, some people rushed the stage. For Gregory's role in the protest, the administration attempted to expel her, an action she interpreted as somewhat complimentary of her efforts as an activist. "There were hearings on the campus of the people on the campus who had been identified as being a part of the demonstration. And there was a lot of reporting in the media about it. So that was an energizing event as well."[92] She perceived her election as queen as having sparked important dialogue that made a larger portion of the student population more interested in the movement. Gregory asserted, "We were trying to focus on things that we thought were important issues that the sleeping middle-class students of Howard University should wake up to."[93]

Ebony's multipage spread, "New Trend Towards Black Beauties: Darker Girls Are Winning Bids for Titles," announced that white college contests were echoing the diversity trend in pageant contests. "Lois Laurin Johnson, a chocolate-brown student of 18, was selected by her schoolmates at Girls' Polytechnic High School to become the first Negro princess in the 60-year history of the Portland Rose Festival—one of the region's largest tourist attractions drawing over half a million annually, rivaling California's Tournament of Roses." It said about 1967, "This fall there was a virtual epidemic of Negro homecoming queens at large schools with a proportionately small Negro enrollment. Some of the largest, like the University of Michigan and the Chicago Circle branch of the University of Illinois awarded crowns to Negro girls." It called nineteen-year-old Daphne Maxwell's win at Northwestern University in Illinois "an unexpected triumph."[94] Later known as Daphne Maxwell Reid who played Aunt Vivian on the hit television show *Fresh Prince of Bel Air*, her homecoming win underscored the relationship between the platform of pageantry and bigger opportunities, especially for Black women.

In 1968, another African American woman triggered transformation on a university campus. She eventually became a leading specialist in United States history and African American social movements, a University of Chicago PhD and chairwoman of the Department of History at Howard University. Different from Robin Gregory, Genna Rae McNeil stirred change at a predominantly white campus. Kalamazoo College, a tiny private liberal arts school in Michigan, recognized its first African American queen with her election just after the assassination of the Reverend Dr. Martin

Luther King Jr. African American students on white college campuses faced perplexing experiences. About white students, McNeil shared:

> *Some of them avoided me. They just didn't want to be bothered. Others thought you were peculiar and they wanted to find out how peculiar you were. Some thought it was a test of their faith and everything else that they had to have you for a roommate. Some were just mean and nasty. By the time I got a really mean and nasty one, I had figured out how I was going to handle things.*[95]

The daughter of pastor and educator Jesse Jai McNeil Sr. (PhD, Columbia Teachers' College of New York) and Pearl Lee Walker McNeil (an anthropologist and human rights advocate with degrees from Fisk University and American University), Genna had been adequately prepared to encounter racism. Her parents instilled valuable lessons on the Black past that gave her self-worth and the spiritual and intellectual wherewithal to remain unbothered and durable, particularly in the face of petty discrimination. She negotiated space with her cantankerous white roommate with stern conviction and a fishnet barrier:

> *You're in a room. It's got two beds, there's very little space and there's one bathroom and, you know, you have to walk past this person's bed…to get to the bathroom and things like that, and seems like there was nothing you could do that was acceptable or whatever….I put a fishnet between my bed and her bed and I said, "That's your half, this is my half. You don't need to speak to me. I will go use the bathroom when I want to. You'll go use the bathroom when you want to, and we just don't need to speak, and that's that"….She complained about stuff every day, all the time, and so finally I said, "You know what? I don't like being with you anymore than you like being with me."*[96]

Despite the dynamics of the situation, McNeil was resolute. She mused, "'Well, if I can't move, you're not gon' make my life miserable,' so I hung up the fishnet and that was that."[97] She found peace and friendship with the few other African Americans on campus and white members of the band with which she traveled and sang during her time there. The growing tide toward Black consciousness transformed her young adult years, as it did for many other students across the country. After a study abroad trip to Germany, she recalled, "When I left I was Negro, when I came back I was Black." The shifts in political articulations had caused major changes in how African Americans chose to identify themselves. McNeil said, "At Kalamazoo College, we still respectfully used the word 'Negro' and 'Negro history' and all that kind of thing." However, by the time she returned, so accustomed to using "Negro," she said she and others would have to remind themselves to use the new term, "Black." In the midst of the sweeping changes, she was reconciling her place within the movement. She thought:

> *I wasn't a militant person. I was trying to navigate my sort of upbringing as a Christian integrationist, but pro–Black struggle person with the Black Power emphasis moving toward Black nationalism....It was easy to move in that direction because you began noticing all the things that were so wrong about the school. No Black professors, no Black history, nothing to recognize Black history month—all those kinds of things—so it was up to the students to push for that sort of thing. We had whites that supported us and were glad about the things we did, and there were many that did not.*[98]

McNeil decided that, although she was part of the Black student movement, she was not going to leave her integrated band because she enjoyed it and understood its significance as a cultural necessity. Black music was important to the campus because students, African American and Caucasian, appreciated it and went to parties specifically for soul and R&B. McNeil often performed Minnie Riperton, Aretha Franklin and Dionne Warwick material. She said, "Being in the band, I got visibility that I wouldn't have had by being just a Black student because, yes, you stuck out, but that didn't mean people wanted to know your name or anything like that."[99]

With the prominence her music act brought, students launched a protest around her personality, similar to Robin Gregory's campaign at Howard. McNeil remembered:

> *They came up with the idea, especially after Martin Luther King was assassinated, that the school was just backward. They said it was ridiculous the school didn't have any Black professors....It was ridiculous they didn't have any Black history. It was ridiculous that Black students had to march and demonstrate for every little thing. So some of my band members along with some of their friends and Black student movement people decided that they were going to fix Kalamazoo College and that they would all vote for me for homecoming queen....As their* [the student cluster] *protest*

of how they [the school] *refused to validate anything Black they were going to elect me homecoming queen and say well we can't get a class* [Black history] *in here immediately and we can't immediately hire a Black professor, but we have control over who is homecoming queen.*[100]

Antiwar sentiments and Dr. King's assassination in 1968 stirred the country. McNeil described hearing shrieking and wailing from students running outside after hearing the news of King's death. In the aftermath, she said Black nationalist sudents, mostly younger African American freshman, were sad and angry. They left the campus and went to Western Michigan University, which had a higher African American population, to be with other Black students. However, she chose to stay on campus to sing at an impromptu memorial service at which she was asked to perform. She shared, "I think I might have sung 'Sometimes I Feel Like a Motherless Child.'" The song dates back to slavery and gained popularity with non-Black audiences

Bethune-Cookman College in Daytona Beach, Florida. Students crown the homecoming queen, circa 1940. *Florida Memory/State Library and Archives of Florida.*

when the Jubilee Singers of Fisk, a Black university in Nashville, performed it on national and international tours. It took on an even deeper meaning during the civil rights era when artists such as Mahalia Jackson, a favorite of Dr. Martin Luther King's, reinterpreted it for contemporary audiences. After McNeil's performance, she wanted to leave for Detroit and be with her family but could not because of widespread rioting that came after Dr. King's murder. Furthermore, Kalamazoo's administration was charged with "thinking the only people who can be identified as beauty and homecoming queen is a white person." Students capitalized on the energy of the era and decided "we were going to tell them 'no.'" McNeil revealed that she was shocked after finding out that she had beat the typical blond competition.

> *To me, it symbolized that they were affirming that it was time for the school to understand that it was no longer appreciated or acceptable for them not to have something that affirmed African Americans' rights, and African American history, and that African Americans were equal and worthy like anybody else. That's what it meant to me. And they were very proud of themselves that their class was the class that was able to have the first Black homecoming queen....I had to represent the entire Black race. Nobody could've told me I was doing anything different from that. I was representing every Black person in the world practically by being homecoming queen. That was a big thing on my shoulders. Singing perfectly, representing race, speeches, what I wore...*[101]

Doby Flowers's 1970 story resembles the pattern of resistance among Black student groups. She, too, experienced racism. A portion of what she endured came from a teacher who blatantly described Black women as more manly than whites. At Florida State University, the Black Student Union clarified its stance against this kind of abusive learning environment by launching a campaign for Flowers. She told an interviewer:

> *Fred, my brother, was here two years before and broke the color line athletically and was the second president of the Black Student Union so we were always involved politically. We made a lot of changes in the University as far as diversifying curriculum, as far as hiring African American staff....Basically the Black Student Union—and I was really active in that—one night, I remember John Burt said, "Okay we've broken down every wall except the queen." And he looked at me and said, "Doby, you gon' have to put on some clothes and we gon' run you*

for queen!"…We designed a strategic campaign to win this position. We didn't look at it as a quote "beauty situation." We looked at it as part of being recognized in all segments of this University, and in this country. That Black people were beautiful, that Black people were smart, that Black people were athletic and could achieve in all of these arenas. So that was the pitch. I'm sure that's why the homecoming queen and chief cannot run today, because it was the most politicized homecoming queen campaign ever in the history of the university.[102]

Ebony's coverage of what was happening on campuses around the United States drew attention to the significance of it all by reminding the public of popular culture's historic reinforcement of American favoritism extended to white women. Even literary folklore, like that recorded in "Goldilocks and the Three Bears" and in the famous line of fantasy "Mirror-mirror on the wall, who is the fairest of them all?" identified femininity, attractiveness and worthiness as presumably white attributes.[103] *Ebony* critiqued advertisements that blatantly declared, "Blondes have more fun," and white-run Hollywood, which forced the public's worship of Jean Harlow and Marilyn Monroe as the sole vessels of pulchritude. The improved representation in varied skin tones in college contests, an article stated, "can be measured by the extent to which the successful entrants have looked Negroid instead of merely resembling sun-tanned white girls.…Negro girls of all hues, at last, are being honored."

Doby Flowers's experiences at Florida State University demonstrated the immediate disadvantages of integration. Black students were tolerated but not welcomed. It was understood that Florida A&M University, across the railroad tracks, was for African Americans. Both schools were located in Tallahassee, Florida, a city that had its own sordid past in segregation. It had been a nasty place for people of color.

Years before Flowers's homecoming win, four white men planned and executed the rape of a young Black woman. Armed with guns and switchblades, they approached a group leaving FAMU's Orange and Green Ball. The two males in the FAMU group were forced to abandon the scene, while Edna Richardson escaped, leaving Betty Jean Owens at their disposal. The four white men drove Owens to a secluded area, raped her seven times and bound and gagged her. Predictably, tensions existed between whites and African Americans in the city for years to come. As a college student, Flowers commented, "Not being awarded the homecoming trophy…not being asked to attend out-of-town football games, not being invited to participate in the gubernatorial inaugural parade—that's what it's like to be a black queen at FSU."[104]

By the late 1970s, pageants sponsored by African American schools and organizations remained free from the obstacles of desegregation. They offered a sometimes complicated yet expressly Black aesthetic as the benchmark and continued the tradition of positive affirmation for the young women who participated. Howard University still stood as a flagship for celebrating Black beauty by way of student leadership in campus queens. The school hosted its own conference of queens when it welcomed campus-elects from Dillard University, Xavier, Millgan Lane College, Florida A&M University, Afro Lane College, Morris Brown College, Lincoln University, Morehouse College, Central State, North Carolina A&T, Miles College and Edward Waters College.[105]

More than forty years later, with the 2012 election of Courtney Pearson—a dark brown and full-figured young woman—as the first African American homecoming queen at the University of Mississippi, a school known for its smeared record in race relations, the effectiveness of beauty competition as an unorthodox method of articulating shifts in expanding beauty ideology remained evident. Interestingly, Pearson's crowning not only marked a first for the university, but it also came fifty years after the enrollment of the school's first African American student, James Meredith. In an interview, Pearson shared her thoughts on the change in the racial and cultural atmosphere of the institution. She said, "I definitely do not think that race came up [as a factor]."[106] A friend added that she had no idea that the University of Mississippi had never had a Black homecoming queen before and that it was important that Pearson understood that she earned student support for no other reason than having deserved it. Pearson did reveal that although she heard negative comments about her size, they surfaced after the election and generally came from people not connected with the school. She confirmed, "I'm honestly very confident with the way I look."

The significance of young African Americans, particularly women, in American social movements and visual culture must not be underestimated. Many of the most transformative demonstrations of the civil rights era were launched by Black students. In addition to many other important roles, women helped to activate the optical and cultural changes that embodied the spirit of this period in American history.

Doby Flowers, the first African American queen at Florida State in 1970, sums up the influence of these kinds of campus elections:

Miss Tuskegee Institute Gail Hinton and court, 1968–69. *Archives at Tuskegee University.*

Miss Tuskegee Institute Brenda Dickerson and court, 1970–71. *Archives at Tuskegee University.*

I think during that period change happened faster than any other period we can look back at in the history of even the country. And it was a time when young people really got together and made a difference...because you don't have those other trappings to really hold you back. So I think during that period of time there was a lot of change that happened and we still see the remnants of that today.[107]

Chapter 4

"THIS IS BETTER THAN BEING MISS AMERICA"

African Americans in Mainstream Contests and the Emergence of the Miss Black America Pageant during the Black Power Era

For the Negro woman, who has been as much a captive of the white man's beauty standards as his economy, the very idea of competing for a national crown has placed her in a touchy position." *Ebony* magazine's reporting noted that as college campuses were beginning to welcome coffee-colored women as queens, so were national contests. The improved representation in varied skin tones, an article stated, "can be measured by the extent to which the successful entrants have looked Negroid instead of merely resembling sun-tanned white girls….Negro girls of all hues, at last, are being honored."

Photographers captured Patricia Williams's state of shock, evidenced by a mouth wide open, upon receiving news she had won 1959's Miss Sacramento, a preliminary to Miss America. Catherine Cartwright and Edna Park represented the Bahamas and Nigeria, respectively, in the 1964 Miss Universe pageant. Dorothy Johnson, "an American Negro," represented Idaho in the same contest following the trail of Corrine Huff (secretary to Congressman Adam Clayton Powell), the first entrant, by being a semifinalist. Sonja Dunson, a double-degreed speech correctionist, represented Detroit. Producers crowned pretty, espresso-colored Sarah Pener, a voice major at Eastman School of Music, as 1965's Miss Rochester, another Miss America preliminary.

As more African American women tried integrating pageants beyond those determined by other students, Sheila Poole remembered such an experience entering the first Miss District of Columbia contest, sponsored by Miss America in 1968. She was one of three Black contestants who were classmates. Poole's statement, "I just wanted to get in for us all," symbolized the overarching sentiment of shared purpose characterized throughout the movement. She saw herself as a representative of African Americans, at the mercy of white beauty standards. She recalled the discriminatory undertones of the experience: "First of all I was hippy, and leggy, and tall, flat stomach, not busty, you know. My hair wasn't extremely long. My hair wasn't knotty. It was shoulder length so, you know, I was passable. I was passable in terms of the white constituents. I was passable. I was acceptable, in terms of beauty."[108]

She remembered a popular dancer friend in high school who entered the competition with her. "I don't think they gave her a second look because she did not wear the straightened hair look. She chose an alternative." However, two years later, the friend ran in the Miss Black DC pageant and won. Referring to the outright disapproval of not only African American physical features but also African American culture, Poole expressed how she understood that she was a favored Black participant: "They would do things like…they'd familiarize themselves with your name. Out of, say, one hundred candidates, they'd know your name. That said to me they've singled you out for a reason." She was very aware of the preferences white judges held:

> *My talent was acceptable: I sang. I did not just sing African American songs or R&B. My training was classical, so I would sing classical music. I would sing it for the pageants because I said that is something they will identify with. If I sing one of my local songs, they're gonna turn me away, and sure enough I would sing the nationally accepted songs and I'd be it.*[109]

Poole commented on how her darker-skinned friends felt about her faring better in the competition, stating, "They recognized that sometimes you had to get inside of a thing to help change it."

African American institutions took up the charge of change, too. They, however, committed to erecting literal and figurative stages on which Black women did not have to navigate white culture or conform to their criteria for beauty. African American businessman J. Morris Anderson conceived of and organized Miss Black America after his two small daughters expressed an interest in becoming Miss America. He sought to protest the older contest's exclusion of Black women. With the help of Phillip H. Savage, an NAACP leader, he staged the very first Miss Black America at the

Joyce Warner of Tallahassee, Florida, in 1971. A twenty-year-old junior at Florida Agricultural and Mechanical University, she was crowned Miss Black Florida and represented the state in the Miss Black America Pageant at Madison Square Garden in New York. *Florida Memory/State Library and Archives of Florida.*

Ritz-Carlton in Atlantic City at midnight on September 7, 1968. Savage explained to the *New York Times*, "We want to be in Atlantic City at the same time the hypocritical Miss America contest is being held." The strategic timing successfully drew the attention of like-minded protestors and media reporters who had completed their coverage of Miss America a while earlier.

Although some popular narratives often credit the NAACP solely for the launch of Miss Black America, the National Association of Colored Women's Clubs (NACWC) and other politically inclined groups and individuals were also integral in its coming into fruition. The NACWC advertised heavily for the inaugural event through the pages of the *National Notes*, its official organ. From September 6 through 8 would be, it said, "three big and beautiful days set aside for extolling the beauty of Black Women within majestic Pageantry." Organizers stated that the pageant was "concerned with and is all about Black Beauty. Black Talent. It is all about letting the world know that Black Women are Beautiful and Talented." The "Statement of Intention" read:

> THE MISS BLACK AMERICA BEAUTY PAGEANT—*1968—acclaims, stages, and applauds Black Beauty and parades the Women of Color as a Universal Symbol of Pride.* THE MISS BLACK AMERICA BEAUTY PAGEANT *publicly probes into our women's culture and charts the origin of an unbroken current of intellect, dignity, courage, talent, and elegance: then shifts the current to a week-end "halt" for charging the attention of the world to the variably kaleidoscope Black Women of America. In pageantry, colorful and without ostentation, the Black Woman is projected in all her charm, poise, and beauty. She is crowned to reign as our Queen, be she black, bronze, sepia, or in between.*[110]

Described in the *National Notes* as a "Beautiful and Black Contest and Pageant for and About Black Women," the competition's publicity spared no expression of Black pride—aesthetically, culturally or politically. Promotional materials for the inaugural queen, Saundra Williams, touted her as a nineteen-year-old Philadelphian who "wears her hair natural, does African dances, and helped lead a student strike last spring at her school."[111] After she and a group of friends were barred from dining at a local restaurant, they formed a unit called the Black Awareness Movement to rally against the racist practices of white businesses at large.

Williams, assertive and sharp, amplified the pageant's stance, telling journalists at the Ritz-Carlton Hotel, "This is better than being Miss America. Miss America does not represent us because there has never been a Black girl in the pageant." She suggested that positive Black images were necessary for African American women, not necessarily to prove anything to white people but as a way to foster positive Black self-images within the Black community. She said, "With my title I can show Black women that they too are beautiful, even with our large noses and thick lips. There is a need to keep saying this over and over because for so long none of us believed it." As common in attempts to improve the whole image of African American women and insert dimensionality into their public identities, scholastic accomplishments, service, activism, personality and even socioeconomic status figured into beauty ideology reconstruction. Williams proudly affirmed that, with her father as an electrical engineer, she was the daughter of "middle-class Negroes" and had worn her hair natural long before it was popular to do so. Her adaptation of the style stemmed from having to one day wash it herself because of her beautician's absence. She matter-of-factly stated, "I just let it dry without doing anything to it. I liked it that way."[112]

NACWC cemented its commitment to developing young African American girls and encircling them in atmospheres of affirmation and maintaining youth-focused initiatives beyond Miss Black America. NACWC ensured that the beauty message covered health, decorum and intellectualism—not merely looks. Known for its work in voter registration and anti-lynching, the nationally active band of women held its "First Debutante Presentation," in which twenty-one ladies from seventeen states participated. Categories for judging included "Charm and Poise, Mental Alertness, Physical Attractiveness, Talent, and Record of community service in club work."[113] Service again appeared as a mainstay in activities encouraged for youth when the Lucky Star Girls Club of Newport News, a NACWC youth affiliate, "made beautiful stuffed animals for the children at the Petersburg Training School at Petersburg for Christmas. Adults and girls' clubs packed several large boxes of clothing, toilet articles, jewelry and a great variety of useful gifts for the girls at the Janie Porter Barrett School for Girls at Peaks, VA for Christmas cheer."[114] The NACWC also commissioned the Junior Women's Clubs of Alton, Illinois, to give baskets to needy families in the area and deliver gifts to patients at the state hospital.[115] The mission of developing young women ran parallel to NACWC's other concerns of civil rights and community outreach. Throughout the year, the Northeastern Federation alone contributed significantly to the underprivileged of Mississippi and collaborated with the Red Cross. The Washington and Vicinity Federation carried out the

May Court at Bragg Stadium in Tallahassee, Florida, in 1959. May Day Queen Delores Ann Bright reigned over traditional May Day festivities sponsored by Leon County schools. Sharing the throne with her was Jimmy Ray Burke, who reigned as king. *Florida Memory/ State Library and Archives of Florida.*

organization's charge to support the academic pursuits of young women as they planned for their upcoming Annual Scholarship Luncheon in Washington, D.C.

Its "Youth Night" in August featured an oratorical, talent and fashion contest awarding winners from St. Louis, Milwaukee, Charleston, Tulsa, Mobile and other cities.[116] National president Myrtle Ollison greeted the Starlettes of the National Association of Girls Clubs, an outgrowth of NACWC for girls from eleven to fourteen, at their meeting, where plans were made for their "Back to School Fashion Show" on October 20, 1969. In addition to forming a dance group within the club, the girls were also "given lessons in charm by Miss Betty F. Chambers of the De Vou School of Charm." A report stated, "The girls are being taught to stand, sit, and bend with poise. Proper attire and proper diet were also discussed. At future meetings other phases of charm will be taught."[117] NACWC, and institutions like it, offered African American girls formal etiquette training they could not likely find in other venues, especially at a rate affordable for most Black parents. The organization continued offering these kinds of opportunities to practice finer womanhood and combined them with Black-centered educational experiences. One such instance was the 1969 Annual Tea and Negro History Program for the Youth of Saginaw given for the Girls Club of Saginaw, Michigan, another youth extension. Dr. Rosa L. Gragg, president emeritus of NACWC, keynoted the theme, "Youth in Action for the '70s."[118]

The association made sure to focus its attention on not just one age group. Its La Servio Juniorettes sponsored a Snow Ball Queen Coronation held at the Holiday Inn of East St. Louis, Illinois. Girls ages five through ten were queen contestants, and their escorts were the same age. The entire family and neighborhood found recognition in NACWC's announcement that Miss Dierdre Powell, six, daughter of Mr. and Mrs. Theodus Powell of 788 Vogel Place, East St. Louis, was crowned Snow Queen.[119] The record of developmental activity continued as the organization hosted a mother-daughter tea in January 1974[120] and held a "Pre-Debutante Tea" in East Chicago, Indiana, in April 1975 at the Knights of Columbus Hall. It presented fifteen girls to society and awarded $1,500 in scholarships.

The NACWC by 1975 again employed pageantry as a device for practicing charity and social welfare when it sponsored the Virginia Youth Miss Teen America contest. The organization presented Angela Riddick, of Chesapeake, Virginia, her crown, a scholarship and a vacation at the Virginia State Federation of Colored Women's Clubs sixty-seventh annual convention in Hampton. The pageant found itself among other conventions, events and assemblies addressing current pressing issues for African Americans, such as the economy and penal system. Roy D. Hudson, president of Hampton Institute, presented "Reaching Out, Reaching Down, and Lifting Up" as his formal address.[121]

As earnest as NACWC's intentions to promote authentic images of Black women were, it repeated the same practices of some other African American organizations that, for financial reasons, accepted advertisements from non–Black owned companies. Many white beauty companies peddled marketing tactics expressly aimed at Blacks. They sought to capitalize on consumer behaviors stimulated by cultural trends of the Black Power era. NACWC's *National Notes* ran the following campaign message from Clairol cosmetics and hair care company intentionally using an African American model to sell its products: "This is the age of Black beauty. Your hair crowns your overall appearance and should be carefully styled and cared for to create your best beauty look. Regardless of your hair trend—whether you express yourself with the natural look, pressed hairstyles or a little of both—your hair must look perfect…Black IS beautiful…so follow these grooming tips, and keep it that way!"[122]

Although non-Black advertisers infiltrated Black publications, African American pageants maintained ownership of themselves as business entities and continued revering Black women throughout the 1960s and 1970s. In June 1969, the Miss Black New Jersey beauty pageant did so as a preliminary to Miss Black America, which was staged at Madison Square Garden.[123] In July 1970, three Cleveland-area, Black-owned and Black-operated companies—American Dream Soap, Super Jet Markets and J&B Photo Studios—joined together to sponsor the American Dream Girl pageant. Organizers stated:

> *The main purpose of this pageant is to display the concern that Black companies have for the further education of youth and the need for educational assistance to be aided by Black businesses which have entered into the mainstream of the American Economic System through the benefit of higher education and a relentless determination and dedication committed to the involvement of Black business in the present capitalist structure.*[124]

Open to all Ohio residents, the contest offered a two-year tuition scholarship to Cuyahoga Community College.

In Philadelphia in 1972, a coalition of citizens organized the area Political Beauty and Talent Pageant. The contest was created to "help develop young women in their political self-sufferances and self-respect."[125] Founder and director Earline J. Williams introduced young ladies, from fifteen to twenty-one, to activities and programs that exposed them to the political affairs of the city for a year before enabling them to compete for the crown. Similarly, the 1972 Miss Black Chicago, another Miss Black America preliminary, grew as a result of coalition building among Black businesses and community leaders. Producers underscored the importance of holding it "in a Black-owned environment."[126] It offered a $7,000 to $10,000 scholarship to Southern Illinois University at Edwardsville, a trip to Nassau, Bahamas, a $100 shoe budget and a cassette tape player, among other prizes. Local girls enjoyed comparable affirmation and recognition, as evidenced in the Miss Watts beauty pageant of 1977, which was aired on KTTV Channel 11. The mission read congruently with others: "To promote trust and understanding, develop community commitment, and awareness, encourage self-improvement of young females in our community."[127] In September 1977, NBC aired the Miss Black America pageant, just one day prior to CBS televising Miss America. Plans for the 1979 Miss Black Universe beauty pageant typified the diasporic consciousness of the era with its focus on

African, European, South American and Caribbean countries. The pageant endeavored to recognize "the ethnic and cultural heritage of the sponsoring nations."[128] By 1979, African American pageantry had commanded the attention of official state leadership, even in formerly segregated states. Georgia governor George Busbee, in an official letter from his office, wrote to Marion Moore, Miss Black Georgia: "Viewing one's self in a positive way is essential in becoming a self-confident individual." Governor Busbee also stated that Moore's role in fostering "the betterment of womanhood is a commendable gesture."[129] Musical artist Curtis Mayfield congealed the trends in Black pride and adoration for Black women with his 1970 cult classic "Miss Black America," in which he crooned:

> *Sisters, we're all so very proud*
> *Of that natural look we see among the crowd*
> *Worldwide admiration*
> *From nation to nation*
>
> *They love you, Miss Black America*
> *We love you, too, Miss Black America*
> *You're such wonderful people*
> *And so beautifully equal*
> *Miss Black America*[130]

Chapter 5

"STEPPING OUT INTO FINER WOMANHOOD"

Football Classics, Coronations and a Local Civil Rights Legend Training Queens in Respectability and Representation

Historically, Black pageantry merged the tasks of affirming Black beauty and affording personal development education to young women from varied backgrounds. Throughout the twentieth century, middle-class African American educators and organizers who oversaw such pageant enrichment programs held to racial uplift as a personal and professional obligation. They addressed the need to cultivate behaviors advantageous to social, economic and even political success in American society. They also forged spaces of aesthetic freedom, without the self-consciousness often caused by the white gaze. Sheyann Webb-Christburg's life's work envelops these ideals.

Consistently adorned with pearls, delicate makeup and hair styled in a classic chignon, Sheyann Webb-Christburg is a social influencer who embodies the instructional dynamics of Black beauty culture as modeled throughout her career. As founder, director and owner of KEEP (Keep Entertaining Everyday People) Productions Youth Development and Modeling Program, based in Montgomery, Alabama, her story bridges the memories of the civil rights movement and the enduring need to mentor young people and provide spaces of aesthetic freedom and beauty affirmation. In addition to overseeing K.E.E.P. for more than thirty years, Christburg authored the book *Selma, Lord, Selma*, which Disney transformed into a movie of the same name. The book and movie are based on her childhood in Selma, Alabama, at the height of national turmoil. They retell her story as a nine-year-old who was playing outside with her friend

Community activist and style influencer Sheyann Webb-Christburg. As a nine-year-old, Webb participated in the first attempt at the Selma to Montgomery march across the Edmund Pettus Bridge on March 7, 1965, known as Bloody Sunday. *Christburg private collection.*

Rachel when they noticed several nicely dressed Negro men drive up to Brown Chapel AME Church. One of the men introduced himself as Martin Luther King Jr. The others simply explained to the girls that they were in Selma to help Negro people get voting rights. With her interest spiked, precocious Sheyann regularly sneaked out of her house to attend the mass meetings about these issues that seemed to have the whole community gripped. Early on, she understood the significance of disenfranchisement, and she is recorded as the youngest person to attempt the 1965 march on Edmund Pettus Bridge. Running into tear gas and seeing law enforcement beating demonstrators with clubs and trampling them with horses, she began to flee and was rescued by the Reverend Hosea Williams. She earned "King's smallest freedom fighter" as a nickname around the small town and led the congregation at Brown Chapel in singing freedom songs like "Ain't Gonna Let Nobody Turn Me Around."

Having sensed the embrace of Selma's community as a youth, Sheyann entered church pageants, Elks Club beauty contests and the Little Miss Fashionetta competition sponsored by Alpha Kappa Alpha sorority. As an adult, Christburg identified such experiences as critical moments of development, which offset the trauma she witnessed during the violent national crisis in her hometown. She remembered, "Being poor, it [involvement in extracurricular beauty and talent activities] really paid off." Her proximity to the movement and the benefit of performing arts and pageantry spawned a desire to provide similar opportunities to young people. Christburg shared:

> *I've always liked to work with young people, particularly young women. Growing up poor and in the projects, those kinds of outlets gave me advantages that have been helpful throughout my entire life. Because of*

Miss Bethel AME Church contest in Tallahassee, Florida, 1954. Identified in the photograph are (*left to right, standing*) Augusta Ford Nims, Mrs. Emma Lincoln, unknown, Annie Tanner, Carolyn Harris and Inez Jones and (*seated*) Mrs A.E. Martin, Zelma Harris, Mrs. C.B.N. Daniels, Mrs. Lillie F. Davis and unknown. *Florida Memory/State Library and Archives of Florida.*

> *those great women, role models, who touched my life and made a tremendous difference, I desire to re-invest, especially into those who are underprivileged, and that's why I founded KEEP Productions.*[131]

Later, Christburg worked in the Office of Development at Alabama State University (ASU), the Black college in Montgomery where faculty and students were instrumental in the famed 1955 bus boycott launched after Rosa Parks's arrest. While at ASU, Christburg raised scholarship funding for students for several years. Most representative of her focus on young women, however, was her role as the official advisor and coordinator for Miss Alabama State University and Court. Christburg repurposed her official role at the university to include formalizing a grooming and empowerment program. Since 1990, she has deposited her leadership in style and refinement as advisor to the many young women elected to the court. She reinforced to young ladies under her purview, "It's beyond the crown. The experience of Miss Alabama State University and Court is about building character. When you develop a strong character, it puts the package together." When asked about her vision for the program, she firmly responded:

> *I have worked with these young ladies in an effort to really embrace the ideas that most parents would want for their little girls. And that is to be the best that they can be and do the best for themselves as they matriculate to not only become young ladies in society, but as they follow their careers in life. And in doing that, it's important to embrace the ideas of, number one, having high self-esteem, believing in yourself and breaking out of non-productive patterns. Taking those weaknesses and making those the best strength that you can because I've always believed that there lies great strength in all of us, particularly in our young women. Sometimes we just have to dig deep inside of us and bring out the best in us. One of the ways that I've been able to do that with the young ladies I work with is teaching them first and foremost how to love themselves and feel good about who they are.*[132]

Her decidedness in performing a personal diagnostic with the queens in order to identify strengths and weaknesses supports the idea of achievable beauty through self-evaluation, not racial identity. Christburg repeated that although she often acts as a tough surrogate mother and does not withhold honesty, she prioritizes getting to know them sincerely—their likes and dislikes. She said, "I ask a series of questions. Out of those discussions, I build on the strengths."

> *I do realize that young women have to deal with many challenges, and one of them is how they feel about themselves. That's the first beast that I like to deal with. The first thing is image consciousness. When it comes to being a queen, image is very, very critical in this process because you are a role model.*[133]

Christburg explained how campus pageantry at ASU offers groups of young women the opportunity to transform the anxiety that image consciousness can cause into excitement and eagerness to be seen and appreciated on a public platform. "My favorite memories are the plans for the coronation. It's a big event for the queens which they *all* look forward to [noting campus queens from various organizations, not just the principal university queen]."[134] She said they look forward to the coronation first and then to homecoming (Turkey Day Classic) and Magic City Classic, the long-standing football rivalry between the largest Black colleges in the state—Alabama State University and Alabama A&M University—that averages over sixty thousand in attendance. At each, the queens are presented on the field during halftime and are seated among university VIPs during the game. According to Africa Miranda, Miss ASU 1997, who reigned under the direction of Christburg, "The classic is the Super Bowl of Black college football life, especially for Alabama State. We have some of the biggest classics ever. The Turkey Day Classic was the first classic ever and the longest-running Black college football classic, so that's, of course, the grandmother of them all."[135] Miranda described Magic City as "one that everyone attends." She exclaimed, "There's no showing up in just any outfit. You have to come correct! The people are sparkling!" She called the Labor Day Classic, another well-known affair in Alabama history, "nice because it's not a huge classic. It's more about the family." "There's the parade," Miranda recalled, "and I know for that we wore pants, which we almost had to get a clearance on. I think that was the compromise we made."

Revealing Christburg's emphasis on traditionalism and more conventional notions of femininity, the former Miss ASU remembered, "We were able to do pants for the parade and then a skirt for the game because they still don't like you doing pants at these games, which I still don't understand." Similar conservative guidelines existed at other Black colleges. Trenice Desseray Seniors, who today has owned Celebrity Hair Designs in Tallahassee, Florida, for more than twenty years, held the Miss Florida A&M University 1989–90 title. While calling her experience "a profound turning point," she said the position caused her to reevaluate and transform herself as a young woman because Miss FAMU "set the bar." Seniors continued, "The administrators had a heavy hand, then, in what I did as Miss FAMU. I literally couldn't go anywhere without people recognizing me, and a lot of people were old-fashioned. I couldn't have a boyfriend that they knew of." Her obligation was to the school and required a wholesome image, even in the more progressive atmosphere of the late 1980s and '90s. Seniors shared, "The man who was my boyfriend—he's now my husband—we were at a basketball game, one of the big games they have at the end of the football season. We were walking up the stairs, holding hands, and someone said, 'No, Miss FAMU, no!'" She resolved her understanding of the role in that moment. "I said [to my boyfriend], 'Let my hand go.' From that point on, I realized I had a charge. The administration looks at you, the city, the student body."[136] These

Fans at Bragg Memorial Stadium watching the FAMU homecoming football game in Tallahassee. *Florida Memory/State Library and Archives of Florida.*

recollections speak explicitly to Black holiday practices and enthusiasm, Black interpretations of femininity and virtuousness, as well as Black intergenerational frictions.

According to Christburg, the young women, who may have to concede to dress codes set by elders, do have creative oversight of coronation. "Coronation is their night! It's when their vision gets to be carried out. One theme that I really loved was 'Stepping Out into Finer Womanhood.'" Interestingly, the notion of "finer womanhood" lived resoundingly in the lexicon of many of the early and mid-twentieth-century guideposts of Black women's club movement. She continued, "A young woman should know what it means to step out. That's why when you embrace a theme it needs to have a positive message that can exuberate to the audience, the other young ladies on campus, the little girls who come as queens who have been selected throughout the city." It typically attracts a large community audience and positions regular college girls to be lauded as models for youth. For those reasons, the theme and the visual presentation should be both impressive and meaningful. She said, "That will really strike a chord! There is no better message for that than 'finer womanhood' when it comes to exuding character, integrity and dignity."[137] Africa Miranda compared her coronation experience to the images she saw of African American women on television. "I still love Vanessa Williams to this day because she was the first [Black] Miss America....I love a good pageant, but you are watching it and there is nobody that looks like you and if there is somebody that did look like you in the pageant, they weren't winning." Vanessa Williams, to Miranda, represented an anomaly in a white space. "You couldn't even do those bigger pageants, so it was incredible to think that you can even have something that, even though it's not on the level of Miss America, to know that you can still have that feeling and that experience." Black colleges and their coronations operate as hubs for the regular reverence of, excitement around and bestowing prizes on African American women. Outside of these institutions, it is an infrequent occurrence. Miranda said:

> *Most Black girls don't get to have that. We don't get to have the experience where we get to feel beautiful, and feel special, and be appreciated, and be awarded for that, because everything in this world tells you that you don't match or you don't get to just be celebrated for who you are. It is a very special thing. It is something that I am so grateful for, and I wish it for everybody. It's a really good thing.*[138]

African American institutions' enduring celebration of regular community girls allowed for family members and close friends to share in the experience of queendom as well. For example, in 1981, Vivian Johnson served as the 75th Miss Florida A&M University; thirty-six years later in 2017, her daughter Michelle Marva Johnson was crowned the 111th. For African Americans, these legacies are not only real but carry weight of community investment and commentary. Michelle Johnson, a third-generation FAMUan and Dallas native, remembered, "Even when I was younger, when I was in church, people would say, 'Hey, Miss FAMU!'—and I hadn't even come here yet!"[139] Africa Miranda described her coronation at ASU, attended by her mother, grandmother and great-grandmother, as a beautiful night during which

Miss Tuskegee Institute 1963–64 Eva Baker holds her trophy with pride. *Archives at Tuskegee University.*

one of her special childhood friends, Andrea Anderson, who was also Miss Tuskegee University at the time, performed as part of the evening program.

It was just a great, really, really good night. We worked very hard on the planning and…well, Andrea is a world-class talent, she is a dancer,

Former Miss Alabama State University Africa Miranda. Miranda later became an award-winning actress and singer. She also owns a thriving health and beauty brand. *Miranda Publicity.*

she has danced her whole life with a trophy ballet company, so she had a wonderful performance, so to be able to have someone that I grew up with and I've known Andrea since eighth grade, so the two of us grew up together, we graduated from high school together, and we were both queens the same year, and to have her be a part of that was also very special. Later, my great-grandmother who was just at my coronation a week before, who I was very close to, had an aneurism, and passed. So that was kind of the cloud for me over the rest of my year, and my reign, but I would say the next great moment was Turkey Day Classic. I am from Montgomery, and there is nothing you want more than to be the hometown girl brought on the field at halftime, so…it was a great day, and really good weather. That, for me, was a great ending to the year.[140]

Being the hometown girl did not necessarily ease the weight of expectations set by court directors. Carrying out responsibilities attached to public engagement, according to Christburg, required not only the presence of durable self-esteem but also self-awareness and consciousness of one's constituency. Mastering all of them at once is a performance art the position teaches. Christburg confirmed, "Miss Alabama State University's title is very critical to the campus and the community. Number one, she is the ambassador. She is the person who is the role model for the students, the campus, the staff and the faculty." Christburg intimated that the queen must fulfill the expectations of her immediate and surrounding network. "When she walks into events, the first thing people see is a queen, and they want to see a queen that looks like a queen, that acts like a queen." As an institutional representative, "she's got to be the example and the role model that people expect for her to be." Miss ASU and court must not only attend a majority of official university functions on and off campus, but in many instances, Miss ASU is also required to speak from the dais. "She has to do introductions of prominent dignitaries or well-known figures. It is so critical for our queens to understand protocol and etiquette. Sometimes queens find themselves in places that they never thought they'd be."[141] Miranda's memories concur:

> *It is much more than what I thought it was. I thought, "I'm just gonna win, I'm gonna go to a couple games, and that's it." It was much more responsibility. I had an office, and I was like, "What am I doing here?" But you just realize that you have things that you are responsible for, accountable for, that had to be done, and at the end of the day when they were looking for Miss ASU, you had to be there, but you still had to get your school work done, and to be in* Ebony *and have little kids writing you. I had people writing from around the whole country, I had some prison letters.*[142]

Miranda still appreciates her appearance in the national magazine. "Every Black college queen gets to be in *Ebony* magazine. If you are Black, you have done something right in your life to make it to *Jet* or *Ebony* or both!" She regarded it as a "huge deal" and received letters from all sorts of people, including little girls who shared their admiration. "It was overwhelming, and you realize the responsibility that you have." The former school queen also summarized how the reign can be challenging as a young person frequently facing scrutiny from alumni and others while balancing cost concerns. "You have a budget that you are responsible for that has to be spread out and spent, and it has to cover yourself. You have the attendants to think about and the responsibilities of the school…things that they ask of you, financial commitments that you have to make on a personal level that the school doesn't pay for." She added, "The school expects you to dress a certain way and look a certain way, but they don't pay for it, so it is a lot of work. And you know, being nineteen at the time, it lends more responsibilities of an individual than you have ever had. That I never had by that point." Miranda described another Miss ASU, Eva Kennedy, as her barometer for success in the position. "She was six feet tall, chocolate skin, short hair. Back in her day, she walked on campus with a fur coat. She is the same to this day. They call her Eva the Diva, and she was the standard by which all Miss ASUs were measured." For Miss ASU, as an official representative of the university, major university functions such as Founders Day required quality wardrobe. Eva surpassed expectations and dazzled audiences in her furs. "For anybody that comes [dignitaries and such], you are a part of the welcoming party. You represent the school at the major football games, so from head to toe you have to have that look, greeting fans, the whole thing at the games."[143] Sometimes off-campus community activities still demanded upscale attire. While queens avoided race as an obstacle in African American pageantry, lack of resources could certainly function as a hurdle.

Furs, however, failed to complete the Christburg package of social success. She clarified, "Queens must know the types of things to say to people who they don't know who are prominent. And even those people that you do know—how to approach them in different settings. These are things that you learn in this capacity, and it can take you a long way in life."[144] The art of conversation and effective communication in a variety of circles proved essential to Miss ASU's obligations. These soft skills, Christburg taught, must be matched by an appropriate appearance, beyond wardrobe, to excel in the queen position. "Hair is very critical because you know we have different kinds of queens come in with different kinds of hair from natural to perms to now weave. And weave can be worn very elegantly, but it has to be the right style." Christburg demands that the style of the hair complement the crown, which is worn at all official functions. The crown, already a glistening showpiece, eliminates the necessity for elaborate hair. "Very simple, very elegant. During coronation time, the nice pinups, the nice elegant pinups, are nice."[145]

Once young ladies conquer self-esteem, self-awareness and consciousness of constituency, the longtime court advisor said that is when they have the tools to embrace the stateliness of the title. "The queen is always the line of demarcation. Sometimes we have shy queens or those with less stage presence. So we put them in situations that really enhance their courage, in terms of the mental aspect, because you have to meet the public." She shared there are many young ladies who come from various walks of life "who come into this role with different ideas, different vision. They come in with a different kind of style....Most times in my role I have to get them to understand the image of a queen and a role model, opposed to their personal style prior to them getting this title. That's one of the transitions that most queens have to understand." Christburg adds, "You have to change what you do in the social lane. You have to step up your game when it comes to character and integrity." Instilling that message into young ladies who have these titles "not only makes a difference in the roles that they play as queen on the campus of Alabama State University, but it takes them a long way in life."[146]

Miranda remembers her director fondly. While the term *southern belle* usually evokes white women's femininity as paramount, Miranda's envelopment in a Black world reset the meaning for her. "My saving grace while being Miss ASU was Mrs. Sheyann Christburg, and if you know anything about queens in Montgomery or ASU or just about beauty in the South, it's Sheyann. Sheyann is the quintessential southern belle." The elder mediated the relationship between the school and the young queen. She taught Miranda the pitfalls to avoid and what opportunities to seize. She told Miranda, "You have to realize this is bigger than you and you have a really big responsibility. Things that you are used to doing, that you want to do, like going out, hanging out," she said, "you can't do that anymore. You have to pick carefully the people who are around you."[147]

Christburg takes pride in mentoring and serving as a tangible example. "As your advisor, if you see me step up my game in terms of how I present myself around you, then yours needs to be taken another two or three steps higher. Anytime I position myself with young ladies and queens in any capacity, I'm going to always, before I walk out of my door, be very cognizant of how I look—from head to toe." She stands by her expectations and her skill in getting young people to embrace them. "I will tell you, every time they step out under Mrs. Christburg, they've been right! I believe in simplicity with elegance." She advises that while young people enjoy trends, in an official capacity as queen, they must prioritize time and place. "Keep it business and conservative. You have to think conservative because you have to think about the crown, you have to think about the sash, you have to think about the jewelry, all of the accessories." Her commentary speaks to her rearing in the small town of Selma and the codes of respectability the civil rights era enforced on women especially. She always considered student budgets and remained open to hearing their perspectives. "When you are limited in funds, it makes it even better. I take pride in going out shopping and working with queens on wardrobe. I have an open ear." She added, "I like to give them opportunity to go with me and look at some things for themselves and get an idea of what they think. And sometimes it works and sometimes it doesn't, but it works either way as a teachable moment." Still, she promoted the idea of pearls because "pearls never really go out of style. I wear pearls a lot for myself, but pearls now can be worn by teenagers and young ladies who are queens in college, any age. Pearls add an elegance to whatever you are wearing." She noted black as one of the official university colors of ASU and a hue she often wears in the form of a classy skirt suit. "Oh, pearls set so beautifully and elegantly with it [the color black]!"[148]

For Christburg, "body choreography" finished the queen's "packaging" process that began with hair styling, attire and pearl accessories. She continued to emphasize these impression enhancement strategies as useful and enduring tools.

> *The young lady needs to learn how to sit like a queen. This will carry you through life. It's two or three different ways that one can sit. When a young lady sits very elegant with her legs together, and sometimes it can be in a cross position and sometimes it does not have to be in a cross position, the hand position makes a difference. The shoulder position can make a difference. Normally, I teach queens to place their hands on their right leg and one hand on top of the other, closed fingers. That's an elegant posture. I teach that to the debutantes that I work with too! What it does is, it lifts you up. When you posture yourself in this position it lifts you in body, spirit and mind. When you are positioned that way, and dressed well, you start feeling good. That's something you can carry for life.[149]*

She continued, "I've always believed in continuity, choreography." Again, the queen's presence should be distinctive from others. To accomplish this, "*Whenever* a queen steps out, particularly if she's in escort position, I think it needs to be choreographed in a way that when people see it, it stands out." She visualized "three beautiful ladies standing there, tall, correct, with their legs in a certain position, shoulders up—exuberating high self-esteem and the beauty that people will see that will make *them* want to be a queen and want to look good." She then described, "When you see those young men

Josephine Merritt crowned Miss Tuskegee Institute at a formal ceremony in 1960. *Archives at Tuskegee University.*

standing with their shoulders up and they are in a certain posture with them [the queens] in a very courtly way, that brings even more attention to them [the queens.] And all that is just about striving to be the best you can be."

As beauty and comportment curators like Christburg managed how young ladies interfaced with the public in style, body choreography and verbal communications, the cultural traditions of the institutions at which they worked ensured and continue to ensure public service is taken seriously and seen as almost mandatory, above notions of typical beauty. After reigning as Miss ASU, Miranda, caramel-colored and quite modelesque, went on to work as a successful singer, beauty expert, event host and commercial and print model (featured in advertisements for Coca-Cola, Crème of Nature, Mary Kay Cosmetics and more) in large part because of her looks. However, she said her face was not enough to secure the crown at ASU. "If you were just a cute girl but didn't make an effort to connect to people, you weren't going to win." In most campus pageants, students, not a panel of random judges, vote. Especially since college campuses tend to hold a surplus of attractive women, candidates must maintain particularly healthy rapports with their peers *before* elections. Prettiness alone falls short. With that and personal branding in mind, Miranda implemented her Miss ASU campaign to focus on health and wellness and performed blood pressure checks for the student body. The enduring presence of community uplift as part of these exercises can be evaluated through the retrospective lenses of turn-of-the-century race work, the Black women's club movement and the broad Black Liberation struggle. Accordingly, African American pageant production is influenced by and reflective of the protracted Black American experience.

Chapter 6

"BLACK BEAUTY WINS EVERY YEAR"

*Miss Black USA's Founder and the Lasting Legacy
of African American Pageants*

Today, the culture of historically Black colleges and universities still promotes the importance of racial uplift work and encourages faculty and students to be of service to their communities. Queens, especially, are expected to serve in such capacity. Throughout her reign, Brittany Brooks, Miss Howard University 2008, collaborated with corporate groups to provide support to students. Brooks organized seminars with the support of a local D.C. firm to educate students about real-estate management and how to secure successful mortgages. She also partnered with Bally Total Fitness to promote healthy living and invited PNC Bank, where she was employed, to Howard to offer instruction on building solid credit. Additionally, she disclosed, "I also did a high school tour with my Mr. Howard [Mr. Howard University, the male counterpart to the "Miss" title] to encourage younger students to go to college."

Cultural continuity factors heavily into traditions of pageantry within Black spaces, especially in the South. Racial identity, solidarity and fluency influence the ways competitions transpire. Africa Miranda recalled during her campaign period saturating ASU with fliers cut out in the shape of the African continent. It was a darling strategy to guarantee people remembered her first name among other candidates, but more than that, it symbolized how cultural continuity coalesced in the hip-hop era and manifested itself on Black college campuses in 1997, the year of Miranda's term. The decade, for young African Americans, was accentuated by music, fashion and film that embraced and rejoiced in African identity.

Hip-hop artists gave themselves African monikers and rapped about the Motherland, while Cross Colours, an urban clothing company, propelled to international fame implementing branding schemes that often included silhouettes of the continent and bold displays of red, black and green, the colors of the Black Liberation flag. During these years, the biographical movie *Malcolm X* introduced and repopularized the life and career of the activist and captivated youth with his revolutionary persona. The decade also produced the hit television show *A Different World*, about Black college life, which featured episodes referencing fictitious campus queen "Miss Hillman College." Miranda's campaign for Miss ASU embodied all of it. She said of her handouts, "Everywhere on campus were red shapes of Africa, green, yellow...AKA [Alpha Kappa Alpha sorority] had green, Deltas [Delta Sigma Theta sorority] and Kappas [Kappa Alpha Psi fraternity] red; gold was for the Ques [Omega Psi Phi fraternity]. We made necklaces out of them like Malcolm X." Much like the Cross Colours fashion, Miranda outfitted her team of supporters in Africa branded shirts. "We were passing out signs, candy. Everybody got something from me or my campaign." She believes that singing, not simply stating, the lyrics to the school song, another instrument of cultural continuity, during the candidates' debate locked in her advantage in the election. "This year the question was 'What's the last stanza of the song and what is its significance to ASU?' It explains the history of the school, so my little thing, rabbit hat trick, was not to just say it, but sing it. So I'm just singing the last stanza and explaining it, and all that was left was the pageant. Did the pageant, and here we are!"[150] She won, hands down.

Some queens point to how these cultural expressions would not work well elsewhere. Adrian Pruett, Miss Howard University 2010 and a successful pageant coach, explained that her close relationships with women who participate in mainstream pageants, particularly in the Miss USA system, provide an opportunity to compare distinctions:

> *I see the differences. Black pageants really propel you to embrace a social responsibility that I don't think most pageants give you. Black pageants expect you to come out strong, know your history and have an action plan for how you want to use that knowledge to make a better path for the men and women that come behind you. It's expected that you come out aggressive with something to say. You're expected to be cheerful and never come out like Black Panther. But it's right on the borderline. You're like the Black Panther wife. You have to embrace your culture and your responsibility toward your*

culture. Just to say, "This is who I am, I enjoy swimming and I like pets" [is not enough]. *That's not to condescend other pageants, but they look for the girl next door, to be sweet and approachable. These pageants want you to be more dedicated.* [151]

Allison Hill, Miss DC International 2012 and a Howard alumna and practicing pharmacist, also chimed in on comparing pageant systems. She said the fraternity to which her father belonged, Omega Psi Phi, formed Miss Black Spartanburg in response to Miss Spartanburg's history of not selecting African American winners. The South Carolina town of Spartanburg once adhered to the policies of slavery and segregation. Many may argue that in some ways, it still does. "Even after Vanessa Williams, they never had Black girls as Miss Spartanburg. You won Miss Spartanburg and then went to [Miss] South Carolina, then you went to Miss America." Hill continued, "They just started within the past few years having Black girls compete. They've never had a Black winner." She described Miss *Black* Spartanburg, however, as family. "It was all about uplift. We built camaraderie and always gave each other constructive criticism. I never won. I did it twice, and I got first runner-up and second runner-up, but I feel like I gained the most from that one." Hill discussed how she so treasured the gifts despite not winning the main title:

> *My favorite prize package was from Miss Black Spartanburg. Because Miss Black Spartanburg is run by a fraternity, they always have the wives make up the prizes. All of the girls who are in the pageant get these huge baskets. They have perfume, towels, sheets, irons, ironing boards and just everything. Everything you need in a college dorm is stuffed in that basket. It wasn't about monetary value, but when I went to college, those were the things I needed. It was special.* [152]

Hill added, "I think Black pageants are always a little more competitive. Like in white pageants, you tend to spend a little bit more money on wardrobe and so forth. But in Black pageants, it's all about that articulation, that self-confidence and elocution." Hill competed in Miss America preliminaries for seven years in North Carolina and Virginia. "I would say in having competed in different pageants, our pageants are a bit more difficult as far as the rules and regulations because we have academic requirements sometimes." As an example, she pointed to Miss Black and Gold National, a well-known Alpha Phi Alpha fraternity tradition. "You have to have like a 4.0 [GPA] and a Miss America–quality talent and be well-spoken. They haven't had a national winner without a 4.0, who's not doing this, this and this, on top of community service." Hill concluded, "Yes, it's refreshing to know our pageants are more competitive sometimes."[153]

Adrian Pruett discussed the difficulty of the National Black College Alumni (NBCA) pageant, also known as the National Black Alumni Hall of Fame pageant. Held by the Hall of Fame Commission, the group hosts events for African American college alumni and leadership. Pruett advised, "They have a trustee board. They give out a lot of scholarships, do programs for current students, and their mission is to ensure the lengthening of the lifespan of HBCUs to make sure three generations from now we will be up and running and still relevant." One of their signature engagements is the queen's competition, held every September with dozens of queens from various HBCUs who compete via extemporaneous oratory presentations. For the Miss Howard University pageant, however, Pruett sang.

> *I sang a medley of Monica's "Silly of Me" and "You're Everything to Me"* [by Denise Williams]. *We blended the old and the new starting with Monica and went back to "…Love, love, stop making a fool of me"* [the original song]. *At Black pageants, your talent should reflect your appreciation for your culture. Lots of people will play classical piano or song, and your audience will be impressed, but even more so when your talent suggests you appreciate Black art and that you don't put it in a category of Black artists as lesser than. You shouldn't at all be afraid to break that.*[154]

Other successful Howard queens have performed Black musical traditions when competing. Kendall Isadore, Miss Howard University 2008 and Miss HBCU 2009, talked about growing up attending predominantly white schools and being one of three African American cheerleaders on her squad in Jonesboro, a suburb of Atlanta. Since, she has become a renowned violinist and used her talent to play both gospel and hip-hop at the Miss Howard pageant. "I played Kirk Franklin's [gospel artist] song "He Reigns" on the violin. So, I walked from the piano to the violin and did that and segued into—at the time, Jeezy's [southern rapper] song 'Put On for My City' was popular. So, I did that at the end." Although she sensed she did well, Isadore was anxious. "If I got nervous at any part in the show, it was probably waiting for the results. We waited for about twenty minutes." She considered the weight

Coveted crown and sash from the Miss Black USA archives. *Miss Black USA Archives.*

of *not* being seen as special because she was Black. "Sometimes I feel like when you're competing against people that look like you, it's even harder because people hold you to a higher standard. I know what it's like to feel like a token because, you know, I've done a lot of violin competitions and all-state and all kinds of stuff." Accustomed to being a "token in those kinds of circles," she rhetorically asked, "How many Black girls play the violin or are classically trained? So, I'm used to that."[155] Still, the night of her Howard pageant, the audience was wowed with her routine featuring an instrument that was usually associated with classical music but in this instance was played to intentionally connect to the sensibilities of a young Black audience, and she won.

Adrian Pruett, crowned Miss Howard the following year, incorporated gospel into her performance to qualify. She explained, "At Howard we have the local school [prerequisite] pageant and the big [university-wide] pageant. Initially, I was in the College of Arts and Sciences and had to go to their pageant. There was maybe ten of us. You submit an application, your GPA needs to be 3.0 and at least be a sophomore." That pageant involved an introduction act with the opening dance, a question-answer portion, formalwear and a talent. Pruett fondly remembered, "I danced to Richard Smallwood's 'Thank You.' I did a liturgical piece. Everybody loved it. It was great."[156]

The African American cultural appreciation found in Black pageants encompasses reverence for the African continent as well. Karen Arrington, founder and CEO of the Miss Black USA Pageant and Scholarship Foundation, in existence since 1984, exemplifies this legacy in action.

For her, Africa is not costume or conceptual but, rather, an indispensable physical, cultural and spiritual factor in establishing healthy Black identity. She proudly shared that after producing Miss Black USA in several U.S. cities over the years, one of her proudest achievements was holding it in West Africa. She said, "To reconnect African Americans to the homeland to the Motherland—that, I think, it just doesn't get much better than that." Arrington expounded:

> *In 2007, we took the pageant to Africa, which no major pageant in the history of this country has ever done. And since that time, we've been covered by the* New York Times, *we've been covered by the* Washington Post, *MSNBC,* Good Morning America, NBC Nightly News, The Monique Show—*we just did an episode with her, and* Tyler Perry *is a sponsor and he affords the young women an opportunity to appear on* Meet the Browns. *So we've gotten some major exposure, but still it's not quite enough because we want to make sure every young Black girl in the country knows that they can be whomever it is that they want to be, and our young women actually demonstrate that.*[157]

Arrington called her memories of Africa "incredible." Being responsible for Black girls' first contact with the continent meant a great deal. "I just remember thinking this is unbelievable. If I told someone this, they wouldn't believe it because these things just don't happen." She said that the local village played music and sang to welcome the young ladies, and in response, they wept. She uttered, "Going to Africa was God's work at that time because it just so happened that that year was our twenty-year anniversary….We went to Gambia, where *Roots* [the 1977 iconic television miniseries about an African American family's journey from slavery to freedom] was filmed." Arrington received a most beautiful and intricate cloth made by the villagers that she holds dear as a source of inspiration. When asked why the time in Gambia was so meaningful, she responded, "It was important for us to go back to Africa because I strongly believe that when we came here our culture was really erased from us." Arrington equates identity with strength and said the pageant participants rediscovered theirs, in large part, because of the international trip. She declared that culturally centered experiences are gateways for self-determination. They allow us, she said, "to define who we are and what we're going to be, and not someone else." Moreover, the diasporic contacts opened opportunities for increased scholarship funding sources and a wider business network. Arrington said, "That year, every single young lady walked away with a scholarship to cover her through a doctorate program. That was incredible." She oversaw thirty-six participants whom she said "didn't go there with that expectation of believing they would walk away with something of that magnitude." She revealed that the offer resulted from the Gambian leadership's awareness of persisting discrimination of Black people in America and their interest in strengthening the connection between Africans and African Americans. She negotiated the scholarships directly with His Excellency and explained that most of her girls were approaching completion of undergraduate degrees.

> *We agreed that we should work out something where the winner would get* [money for] *a graduate degree and that would be something that we could continue to discuss, and he said, "OK, I'll give a graduate degree," and I said, "To the winner?" He said, "No, to all of them." I looked at him and I just cried and I said, "You would give all of my girls a degree?" He said, "Yes." "You would give them a scholarship through a doctorate program?" And he said yes. The tears really started pouring because people don't really know* [the difficulties Black people face]. *But he certainly knows, you know, what we go through in the U.S.*[158]

After having been in West Africa for more than two weeks and receiving considerable media coverage, the Miss Black USA pageant drew the attention of multiple countries. Arrington mentioned, "There were other nations who had come to me and said, 'I would like you to bring the pageant to Egypt...we would like you to bring the pageant to Morocco.' The interactions amplified Arrington's commitment to diversity. In 2010, Nigerian American beauty Osas Ighodaro reigned as Miss Black USA. Arrington boasted, "We have young women who represent all shades all sizes and we celebrate their uniqueness, and that's what's really so special I think about the organization."[159]

When asked about her motivation for founding Miss Black USA, she explained, "Well there was only one national pageant [Miss Black America] at that time for African American women, and it was run of course by a male." She offered, "When males are involved, they bring a different perspective, and I thought being a woman and knowing what it is to live in this world as African women, women should have leadership in this." She also alluded that the 1991 Miss Black America pageant held in Indiana had few boundaries in place between young women

Members
of a Miss
Black USA
group
raise fists
in racial
solidarity at
the White
House in
2016. *Miss
Black USA
Archives.*

contestants and a celebrity guest, famed boxer Mike Tyson. After a date and visiting his hotel room early the following morning, eighteen-year-old contestant Desiree Washington was admitted to a hospital and filed rape charges against Tyson. "Everybody that's been around and knows about the Miss Black America system knows about the Mike Tyson incident. And that really is a sore spot in many people's minds who were around during that time." Arrington said while she appreciated how Miss Black America handled the fallout, she thought, "I never would've allowed that to happen....As women we are conscious of anything that could become a negative in an environment that's focused on women." She expounded, "You are really setting yourself up for a disaster when you allow young men of that stature to come in and have sort of free will with the young women." Quite succinctly, she quipped, "That's not what it's about." She says Black pageant and enrichment systems should empower women. "The values that we instill...the inspiration that we give them to step into their greatness and the responsibility that they understand that they have to give back helps not only the African American community, it helps society as a whole: when we're better, the country's better...we're all better too."[160]

Kalilah Allen-Harris, Miss Black USA 2007, agrees that these programs, when implemented well, have lasting advantages for women and the world. Allen-Harris, an MD from Meharry Medical College whose tuition was covered by Miss Black USA, believes, "Pageants prepare you for life's stage!" She said:

Now, I do not believe in pressuring children. But if a child shows interest [in competing], *encourage it. If a five-year-old can conquer a fear, that's priceless. If that same kid loses and has the wherewithal to come back and try again, that's priceless. Alternatively, if a child wins, that's an experience no one can take away. It makes them believe in possibilities for themselves, and more importantly, it puts the responsibility of outcome, either way, on* them. *It's an early lesson in preparedness and accountability and personal presentation. Those rewards have no ending. Look at how many successful women come out of pageants. It's a particular skill set you hone.*[161]

Again, for the aforementioned women, physical attractiveness appeared as subordinate to the process of perfecting their definition of beauty. Remarkably, *Nefer*, an ancient African concept, in its meaning addressed honor or causing goodness to occur as foundational to any other understanding of beauty. As a prefix, it is attached to the names of famous Egyptian queens, including Nefertiti and Nefertari. By the twenty-first century, Black women in America in the beauty realm also tended to foreground less superficial dynamics: personal development, refinement, societal impact and overall success.

Arrington noted of her childhood, "I thought Harriet Tubman was beautiful. I used to walk around the house and put my durag [head wrap] on and start reciting some of her language." Even then, she said, "I thought beauty was being courageous. I thought beauty was sort of doing something for others. That's how I define beauty. I never saw it as superficial or physically; I always defined it by being courageous and giving back."[162] She confirmed that her early ideas persevered and still shape her vision and management style for Miss Black USA.

However, Black beauty discourse in its present iteration is not without lingering problems stemming from white supremacy, patriarchy and respectability politics. Adrian Pruett, Miss Howard University 2010, revealed one of her first perplexing experiences as Miss Howard was a queens' networking event in Greensboro, North Carolina, near the campus of Winston-Salem University. There, all of the student leaders appointed for the upcoming academic year gathered to learn their roles, set calendars and plan for executing their service platforms. She wore her natural hair to the gathering. Pruett recalled, "My advisor asked me to press my hair

Campus Queens Reunion at Tuskegee Institute in 1981. *Archives at Tuskegee University.*

for that just because we wanted to look polished. It came from a good place. She just wanted me to look good." Nonetheless, Pruett questioned the recommendation. "I kind of challenged the standards of what 'looking best' means." Instead, she sported an afro. She said students "loved it" and "flocked" to her. Other young women confided in her, saying, "My hair is natural too, girl!" When confronted by those who believed the hair that grew out of Black girls' scalps should be somehow altered, Pruett retorted, "I have a problem with that mindset." She smiled contently while thinking about her decision to avoid straightening her hair throughout her reign. She hoped her stance freed others from pressure to modify their natural selves. "You have to be the change you want to see. I was ready to see some girl just love herself and wear what she's got."[163]

Perhaps what makes the tradition of Black pageantry most rousing is its honesty about these issues and its coinciding earnest efforts to unravel and address them without being defined by them. The corresponding discourse also offers a constant stream of appreciation for those who, like Pruett, confront conventional notions of beauty and actively pursue a Black aesthetic. Quite simply, it fosters and directs conversations and relationships, *Black woman* to *Black woman*, without outside curation. By negotiating the dynamics of race, gender and representation exclusively among themselves, this approach guarantees, in the words of Miss Black USA 2016 Tonille Simone Watkis, "Black beauty wins every year."[164]

NOTES

Introduction

1. Chandrika Narayan, "Official Who Called Michelle Obama 'Ape in Heels' Gets Job Back," cnn.com, December 14, 2016, www.cnn.com/2016/12/13/us/official-racist-post-return-trnd/index.html.

Chapter 1

2. "Baltimorean a Prize Beauty: Miss Hazel Macbeth," *Baltimore Afro American*, October 3, 1914, 1.
3. Ibid.
4. Ibid.
5. "Nominees in American Legion Beauty Contest," *Pittsburgh Courier*, August 25, 1923, 9.
6. *The Negro Magazine*, August 1927, cover.
7. "Beauty Pageant to Be Staged by *The Philadelphia Tribune* and the Royal Theater," *Philadelphia Tribune*, July 30, 1931, 6.
8. "MD Misses Ask to Enter Balto Eliminations," *Baltimore Afro American*, August 8, 1931, 13.
9. "Which Style Do You Prefer," *Baltimore Afro American*, August 15, 1931, 9.
10. "A Beautiful Contestant Out to Win 100," *Metropolitan Post*, June 3, 1939, vol. 2, issue 22, 1.
11. "Red Mill Advertisement," George P. Johnson Papers, UCLA-Library Special Collections, Charles E. Young Research Library.

12. "Gary, East Chicago's Big Bronzeville Events Have Many Candidates," *Metropolitan Post,* June 3, 1939, vol. 2, issue 22, 7.

13. "'Miss Bronzeville' Beauty Contest Entry Blanks Must Be in Post Office, June 12," *Metropolitan Post,* June 3, 1939, 9.

14. Ibid.

15. "Glamour Girl of 1938…Gladys Snyder," *Silhouette* (n.d.), 12. George P. Johnson Papers, UCLA-Library Special Collections, Charles E. Young Research Library.

16. [Girl reserve Court of 1939], *Silhouette* (n.d.), 10, George P. Johnson Papers, UCLA-Library Special Collections, Charles E. Young Research Library.

17. "Our History," Miss America Since 1921, www.missamerica.org/organization/history.

18. Nell Irvin Painter, *The History of White People* (New York: W.W. Norton, 2010), 367.

19. Elwood Waltson and Darcy Martin, *There She Is: The Politics of Sex, Beauty, and Race in America's Most Famous Pageant* (New York: Palgrave MacMillan, 2004), 99.

20. Maryrose Reeves Allen, "Master Plan for May Festival," 1940, Maryrose Reeves Allen Papers, Howard University Moorland-Spingarn Research Center, Manuscript Division, Washington, D.C.

21. Ibid.

22. "Gary, East Chicago's Big Bronzeville Events," *Metropolitan Post.*

23. "First Negro Beauty Queen to See Paris," *Jet*, October 28, 1954, 27.

24. Allen, "Master Plan for May Festival."

25. Natasha L. Henry, *Emancipation Day: Celebrating Freedom in Canada* (Ontario, CAN: Natural Heritage Books, 2010), 69.

26. "Shriners Grid for August Meet in New York," *Kansas City Plain Dealer,* July 27, 1951, vol. 53, issue 30, 8.

27. "Koran Temple to Sponsor a Shrine Talent, Beauty Pageant," *Kansas City Plain Dealer,* June 6, 1952, vol. 54, issue 23, 4.

28. Ibid.

29. "Shrine Talent, Beauty Pageant to Hold Spotlight on Saturday," *Kansas City Plain Dealer*, May 8, 1953, vol. 55, issue 16, 6.

30. Ibid.

31. "Biggest Negro Beauty Contest," *Jet*, September 25, 1958, 60.

32. Ibid.

33. "Memphis Cotton Makers' Jubilee Headquarters—Arkansas A&M Co-ed Wins Coveted Title," news release, 1955, Mary McLeod Bethune Papers, Bethune Foundation Collection, National Archives for Black Women's History, Washington, D.C.

34. Ibid.

35. Ibid.
36. The Digital Archive of Memphis Public Libraries, "Dr. R.Q. and Ethyl H. Venson Cotton Makers' Jubilee Collection," memphislibrary. contentdm.oclc.org/digital/collection/p13039coll1/id/39.
37. Mrs. R.Q. Venson, "Special Requisites," from Jubilee Contest and Tour Chairman, 1955, Mary McLeod Bethune Papers, Bethune Foundation Collection, National Archives for Black Women's History, Washington, D.C.
38. Ibid.
39. Ibid.
40. Bale of Cotton: Winners and Prizes, general contest literature and short biographies of selectees, 1955, Mary McLeod Bethune Papers, Bethune Foundation Collection, National Archives for Black Women's History, Washington, D.C.
41. "Society," *Jet*, March 15, 1952, 42.
42. "Omegas Crown Queen," *Jet*, April 21, 1955, 16.
43. "Society," *Jet*, April 10, 1952, 44.
44. "Education: 'Charm' Meets 'Esquire,'" *Jet*, May 21, 1959, 46.
45. Ibid., 44.
46. "Society," *Jet*, February 26, 1952, 44.
47. Ibid.

Chapter 2

48. Audrey Kerr, *The Paper Bag Principal* (Knoxville: University of Tennessee Press, 2006), 83.
49. Ibid.
50. "Are Creoles Negroes?" *Jet*, June 25, 1953, 12.
51. Linda Grace Brown, interview by author, digital video recording, Montgomery, Alabama, December 28, 2010.
52. "The Truth About Beauty Contests," *Jet*, February 26, 1953, 28.
53. "African Queen," *Jet*, April 24, 1952, 17.
54. Ibid.
55. "Most Beautiful Women in Negro Society," *Jet*, December 19, 1953, 44.
56. Sara Maddox, interview by author, digital video recording, Atlanta, Georgia, March 17, 2011.
57. Ibid.
58. Barbara Anders, interview by author, digital video recording, Miami, Florida, March 19, 2011.
59. Ibid.
60. Ibid. See also John Michael Lee Jr., *American Higher Education without Public HBCUs: A Study of Four States* (LAP Lambert Publishing, 2011).

61. Ibid. See also Jennifer Leigh Selig, *Integration: The Psychology and Mythology of Martin Luther King and His (Unfinished) Therapy with the Soul of America* (Carpentaria, CA: Mandorla Books, 2012).

62. Veronica Hicks Gibson, interview by author, digital video recording, Miami, Florida, March 16, 2012.

63. Brown, interview.

Chapter 3

64. Maddox, interview.

65. Ibid. See also JoAnne Robinson and David Garrow, *The Montgomery Bus Boycott and the Women Who Started It* (Knoxville: University Press of Tennessee, 2005).

66. Mona Bethel Jackson, interview by author, digital video recording, Miami, Florida, March 21, 2011.

67. Hicks Gibson, interview.

68. Ibid.

69. Anders, interview.

70. Ibid. See also Douglas Martin, "Patricia Stephens Due Dies at 72; Campaigned for Civil Rights," *New York Times*, February 11, 2012, A28.

71. Diane Bargeman, interview by author, digital video recording, Miami, Florida, March 21, 2011.

72. Ibid.

73. Glenda Alice Rabby, *The Pain and the Promise: The Struggle for Civil Rights in Tallahassee, Florida* (Athens: University of Georgia Press, 1999), 191.

74. Hicks Gibson, interview.

75. Ibid.

76. Anders, interview.

77. Hicks Gibson, interview. See also Elizabeth Clark-Lewis, *Living In, Living Out: African American Domestics in Washington, DC 1910–1940* (Washington, D.C.: Smithsonian Books, 2010).

78. Maddox, interview. See also Hasan Kwame Jeffries, *Bloody Lowndes: Civil Rights and Black Power in Alabama's Black Belt* (New York: New York University Press, 2009).

79. Ibid. See also Barbara Ransby, *Ella Baker and the Black Freedom Movement: A Radical Democratic Vision* (Chapel Hill: University of North Carolina Press, 2003).

80. Annette White, interview, video recording, August 2011, "Albany State University Activists," *World News Inc.*

81. Ibid. See also Henry Hampton, *Voices of Freedom: An Oral History of the Civil Rights Movement from the 1950s through the 1980s* (New York: Bantam Books, 1991).

82. Annette Jones White, "Giving Up the 1961 Miss Albany Crown in the Battle for Civil Rights," *Washington Times-Communities*, January 27, 2013.

83. Robin Gregory, "Interview with Robin Gregory," interviewed by unidentified interviewer, *Eyes on the Prize* television series, Blackside Inc., Washington University Libraries, Film and Media Archive, Henry Hampton Collection, October 12, 1988.

84. Broadus Butler, "The Negro Self Image," *Negro Digest*, March 1962, 68.

85. Gregory, "Interview."

86. Ibid.

87. E. Fannie Granton, "Dark Girl 100th Anniversary Homecoming Queen," *Jet*, November 10, 1966, 48.

88. Ibid. See also Ibram Rogers, *The Black Campus Movement: Black Students and the Racial Reconstitution of Higher Education, 1965–1972* (New York: Palgrave Macmillan, 2012).

89. Gregory, "Interview."

90. Ibid.

91. Ibid. See also Martha Biondi, *The Black Revolution on Campus* (Berkeley: University of California Press, 2012).

92. Ibid.

93. Ibid. See also Stokely Carmichael, *Ready for Revolution: The Life and Struggles of Stokely Carmichael* (New York: Scribner, 2005).

94. "Darker Girls Are Winning in Bids for Titles," *Ebony*, December 1967, 170.

95. Genna Rae McNeil, interview, video recording, Leadership in Grooming and Beauty Culture Collection, National Archives for Black Women's History, Washington, D.C.

96. Ibid.

97. Ibid.

98. Ibid.

99. Ibid.

100. Ibid. See also Taylor Branch, *Pillar of Fire: America in the King Years 1963–1965* (New York: Simon and Schuster, 1998).

101. Ibid. See also Julie Bettie, *Women Without Class: Girls, Race, and Identity* (Berkeley: University of California Press, 2003).

102. Doby Flowers, "Interview with Doby Flowers," interviewed by Suzanne Smith, Florida State University WFSU-TV Issues in Education television series, 50th Anniversary of FSU Integration, April 9, 2012.

103. "New Trend Toward Black Beauties," *Ebony*, December 1967, 164.

104. Bruce A. Thyer, *Cultural Diversity and Social Work Practice* (Springfield, IL: Charles C. Thomas Publisher LTD, 2010).

105. "Black Campus Queens Visit HU," *The Hilltop* 59, no. 24, April 8, 1977, 1.

106. Mark Memmott, "Mississippi Queen: My Race Wasn't a Factor in Homecoming Title," *The Two Way: Breaking News from NPR*, October 18, 2012.

107. Flowers, "Interview."

Chapter 4

108. Sheila Poole, interview, video recording, Leadership in Grooming and Beauty Culture Collection, National Archives for Black Women's History, Washington, D.C.

109. Ibid.

110. "The Miss Black America Beauty Pageant—1968: Black and Beautiful!" *National Notes: Official Organ of the National Association of Colored Women's Clubs, Inc.* 51, no. 2 (September–October 1968): 21, Records of the National Association of Colored Women's Clubs, 1895–1992, National Archives for Black Women's History, Washington, D.C.

111. Judy Klemesrud, "Philadelphian Chosen First Miss Black America," *Eugene Register Guard*, September 10, 1958, Mary McLeod Bethune Papers, Bethune Foundation Collection, National Archives for Black Women's History, Washington, D.C.

112. "Miss Black America Beauty Pageant—1968," 25.

113. Ibid.

114. "Lucky Star Girls Club," *National Notes* 52, no. 1 (January–February 1969): 6.

115. "The Merry Hart Club and the Junior Women's Clubs," *National Notes* 52, no. 1 (January–February 1969): 7.

116. "Youth Night," *National Notes* 52, no. 1 (January–February 1969): 6, 24.

117. "Club News and Views," *National Notes* 52, no. 1 (January–February 1969): 8.

118. "Social Event," *National Notes* 54 (1969): 6.

119. "Young Adults," *National Notes* (September–October 1971).

120. "Debutante Tea Held," *National Notes* (Winter–Spring 1975): 7.

121. "Club News and Views," *National Notes* (Fall–Winter 1975): 6.

122. "To Be Beautiful and Black," Clairol advertisement, *National Notes* 52, no. 1 (January–February 1969): 35.

123. "Miss Black Beauty Pageant in Newark New York," *Amsterdam News*, June 28, 1969, 34.

124. "Three Firms Sponsor Beauty Pageant," *Cleveland Call and Post*, July 4, 1970, 15a.

125. "Political Beauty and Talent Pageant," *Philadelphia Tribune*, October 31, 1972, 7.

126. "Jo Green Vows Greatest Beauty Pageant for 1972," *Chicago Defender*, June 10, 1972, 25.

127. "Miss Watts Beauty Pageant Set at Long Horn Theater," *Los Angeles Sentinel*, June 23, 1977, B5a.

128. "Miss Black Universe Pageant Set," *Cleveland Call and Post*, July 22, 1978, 1B.

129. "Beauty Pageant Hailed by Governor," *Atlanta Daily World*, August 2, 1979, 3.

130. "Curtis Mayfield Miss Black America Lyrics," Genius.com, genius. com/Curtis-mayfield-miss-black-america-lyrics.

Chapter 5

131. Sheyann Webb-Christburg, in conversation with the author, Montgomery, Alabama, January 2011.

132. Ibid.

133. Ibid.

134. Ibid.

135. Africa Miranda, in conversation with the author, Atlanta, Georgia, March 2011.

136. Erin Hoover, "Florida A&M Continues to Honor a Regal Tradition," *Tallahassee*, January 3, 2018, www.tallahasseemagazine.com/January-February-2018/A-Regal-Tradition/index.php?cparticle=2&siarticle=1# artanc.

137. Webb-Christburg, in conversation.

138. Miranda, in conversation.

139. Hoover, "Florida A&M Continues."

140. Miranda, in conversation.

141. Webb-Christburg, in conversation.

142. Miranda, in conversation.

143. Ibid.

144. Webb-Christburg, in conversation.

145. Ibid.

146. Ibid.

147. Miranda, in conversation.

148. Webb-Christburg, in conversation.

149. Ibid.

Chapter 6

150. Miranda, in conversation.

151. Adrian Pruett, in conversation with the author, Washington, D.C., April 2011.

152. Allison Hill, in conversation with the author, Washington, D.C., May 2012.

153. Ibid.

154. Pruett, in conversation.

155. Kendall Isadore, in conversation with the author, Washington, D.C., May 2012.

156. Pruett, in conversation.

157. Karen Arrington, in conversation with the author, Washington, D.C., May 2012.

158. Ibid.

159. Ibid.

160. Ibid.

161. Kalilah Allen-Harris, in conversation with the author, Houston, Texas, February 2018.

162. Arrington, in conversation.

163. Pruett, in conversation.

164. Instagram, @missblackusa, www.instagram.com/p/ BXGQUpEnhOW/?hl=en&taken-by=missblackusa.

INDEX

ABOUT THE AUTHOR

With a terminal degree in United States history from Howard University, Dr. Kimberly Brown Pellum specializes in the history of women's images, southern culture and the Black Freedom Struggle. Her contributions to publicly accessible history include work at the Smithsonian Institution's National Museum of American History, the Rosa Parks Museum and Google's Arts and Culture series. She is the director of the digital archives project TheMuseumofBlackBeauty.com and serves as a member of the history faculty at Florida A&M University.

Visit us at
www.historypress.com